PRESENTED TO

FROM

DATE

HOW TO Read Your Bible & *enjoy it!*

NEW LENSES FOR SEEING GOD'S WORD CLEARLY

How To Read Your Bible and Enjoy It: New Lenses for Seeing God's Word Clearly

Copyright © 2024 Breakfast for Seven

All rights reserved. No part of this book may be reproduced or transmitted in any form or by any means, electronic or mechanical, including photocopying, recording, or by any information storage and retrieval system, without permission in writing from the publisher.

The Introductions of Psalms, Proverbs, Song of Songs, and the New Testament books were originally published by BroadStreet Publishing®, as part of The Passion Translation NT with Psalms, Proverbs, and Song of Songs, this edition is the TPT 2020 edition text, copyright © 2020, Passion & Fire Ministries Inc, translated by Brian Simmons and used with permission.

Scripture quotations marked ESV are taken from The ESV® Bible (The Holy Bible, English Standard Version®), © 2001 by Crossway, a publishing ministry of Good News Publishers. Used by permission. All rights reserved.

Scripture quotations marked NASB are taken from the (NASB®) New American Standard Bible®, Copyright © 1960, 1971, 1977, 1995, 2020 by The Lockman Foundation. Used by permission. All rights reserved. lockman.org

Scripture quotations marked NIV are taken from the Holy Bible, New International Version®, NIV®. Copyright © 1973, 1978, 1984, 2011 by Biblica, Inc.™ Used by permission of Zondervan. All rights reserved worldwide. www.zondervan.com The "NIV" and "New International Version" are trademarks registered in the United States Patent and Trademark Office by Biblica, Inc.™

Scripture quotations marked NKJV are taken from the New King James Version®. Copyright © 1982 by Thomas Nelson. Used by permission. All rights reserved.

Scripture quotations marked NLT are taken from the *Holy Bible*, New Living Translation, copyright © 1996, 2004, 2015 by Tyndale House Foundation. Used by permission of Tyndale House Publishers, Carol Stream, Illinois 60188. All rights reserved.

Scripture quotations marked TPT are taken from The Passion Translation®. Copyright © 2017, 2018, 2020 by Passion & Fire Ministries, Inc. Used by permission. All rights reserved. ThePassionTranslation.com.

ISBN: 978-1-951701-67-3

Produced by Breakfast for Seven
breakfastforseven.com

Printed in China.

*Ears that hear and eyes that see —
the LORD has made them both.*

PROVERBS 20:12 (NIV)

CONTENTS

Introduction vi

PART ONE — 12 Lenses

Read Your Bible ...

#1 In Context 3
#2 As a Redemption Story 13
#3 With an Understanding of the Two Covenants 21
#4 Through a "New Covenant" Lens 37
#5 As a Treasure Chest of Revealed Mysteries 45
#6 As a Son, Not a Servant 53
#7 At the Right "Tree" 59
#8 As Good News 69
#9 As a Love Letter From God to You 81
#10 With "The Helper" — The Holy Spirit 87
#11 Knowing it is Alive and at Work in You 95
#12 With Fresh Eyes and an Open Heart 103

PART TWO — How to Read & Enjoy

Psalms 109
Proverbs 113
Song of Songs 119
The New Testament 124

PART THREE — One-Year Bible Reading Plan

Traditional Reading Plan 252
Chronological Reading Plan 258

INTRODUCTION

"Read your Bible!" It's the first piece of advice most new Christians receive. And it's good advice. And we want to do well in our new faith. So, we read it. But do we enjoy it? Do we go to it for life or for rules for living?

For too many believers, the Bible remains a closed book. They read but find it dry, or even confusing. When handed a new book, our natural habit is to start on page one and proceed page-by-page from there. But what if that isn't the best way to approach the Bible for understanding and light?

The Bible is presented to us as a single book. Yet a glance at the Table of Contents reveals that it's actually 66 books written across roughly 15 centuries. And the fact that those books are divided into two groups, labeled "Old" and "New," is shouting something very important to us. But what?

Why does the God of the Old Testament often seem to have a different personality than the "heavenly Father" presented to us by Jesus and the New Testament writers? Why do the words of Jesus sometimes seem at odds with some statements made by Paul? How and when should we factor in the cultural settings and historic time frames of things that were written 2000, 3000, and even 3500 years ago?

We're told that the Bible is supernaturally perfect. (*Inerrant* and *infallible* are the words usually used to describe this perfection.) And that's true. But that doesn't mean it doesn't need to be interpreted. Varying interpretations are the reason there are so many different denominations claiming contradictory things — and all of them pointing to the Scriptures and shouting, "Can't you see it? It's right here in black and white!"

The problem is most believers aren't given, along with that exhortation to "read it," the tools to do so with understanding. We're not given keys to interpreting it well. What we need is a reliable set of "lenses" that bring the Bible into focus. "Reliable" is the key word there because lenses aren't optional when reading. We all come to the pages of our Bibles with lenses made from what we assume to be true and what we've been told. And these lenses both influence and filter what we "see" and what we *don't* see.

Then there is the matter of translation. You see, the various books and letters that make up the Bible were all written in ancient languages — Hebrew, Greek, or Aramaic — not English. It has to be translated into English, and there are three basic approaches to that important task: word-for-word, thought-for-thought, or paraphrase.

All are valid and beneficial. But there are a couple of challenges built into all of these ways of translating the ancient manuscripts.

First, many Hebrew and Greek words have multiple meanings, just as many of our English words do. For example, the Hebrew word erets (אֶרֶץ) can mean soil, land, region, country, or the whole planet Earth. In a similar way, the Greek word kosmos (κόσμος) can mean the universe, the planet Earth, all the people on the Earth, or an ordered system. So, translators have to look for clues in the context of the passage and make a judgment call about which English word is the best match.

Secondly, translators are fallible human beings. And they bring their own theological assumptions to the difficult process of deciding which English word or phrase to use. This is one reason why it's healthy and helpful to use a variety of translations when studying the Bible.

Your Bible is a wonderful gift from God. Ancient yet eternal. Unchanging yet living and active. Reading the Bible like it fell out of the sky last week, personally addressed to you — without regard to who wrote it, when and why they wrote it, and who they wrote it for — is *a* way of reading the Bible, but it should not be your *only* way.

The following guide is designed to provide you with 12 distinct lenses that can turn the Bible from a mysterious, closed book to a rich, open one for you as a believer. They will equip you to dive into the Scriptures and swim with confidence and joy. You'll also find additional helps and tools for deeper understanding as you study the Bible. May this guide help you discover all the treasures of understanding, light, and life they hold.

PART ONE

12 Lenses

Lens #1

READ YOUR BIBLE

in Context

Reframe it ...

The Bible is a miraculous, wondrous thing. It's a gift from God to us. That means the Bible is for *you* — personally. God wanted you to have it and understand it. And we can be sure that the original writings in the original languages (Hebrew, Greek, and Aramaic) were inspired by the Holy Spirit and communicate exactly what God wanted to say to us.

But, as noted in the Introduction, translation from those original languages is an important but subjective job, done by skilled but fallible people. As also noted in the Introduction, Bible translators often look to the context to decide which English word to use.

> **Context matters. Not just the context around a certain word or sentence in your Bible, but also the bigger context in which each book of the Bible was originally written and read.**

You see, one of the amazing things about the Scriptures is that there is more than one way, or mode, of reading them. For example, because all words from God are alive and active, a scripture can, with the help of the Holy Spirit, speak directly to your specific circumstances. As Hebrews 4:12-13 (TPT) says:

> *For we have the living Word of God, which is full of energy, like a two-mouthed sword. It will even penetrate to the very core of our being where soul and spirit, bone and marrow meet! It interprets and reveals the true thoughts and secret motives of our hearts.*

Countless Christians throughout the centuries have come to the Bible with a specific question, decision, or need weighing on their hearts, opened their Bibles, and found the answers they needed practically jumping off the page.

But there is another, more basic, and absolutely essential way to read your Bible. It is reading "in context." This is vital because, as Paul told his protégé Timothy:

> *God has transmitted his very substance into every Scripture, for it is God-breathed. It will empower you by its instruction and correction, giving you the strength to take the right direction and lead you deeper into the path of godliness.*
> (2 TIMOTHY 3:16, TPT)

So how do you read "in context?" Before interpreting and applying, it is helpful to ask and learn: Who was the inspired writer of this book? Who was it written to? And what was the setting?

Fortunately, many of the best Bibles contain information like this at the beginning of each of the individual books. One of the very best sets of these has been collected for you at the end of this guide. (These are the book introductions written by one of the greatest living Bible translators, Brian Simmons, for The Passion Translation®.) He has not yet translated every book of the Bible, but included here you'll find the entire New Testament, as well as Psalms, Proverbs, and Song of Songs, starting on page 107.

Here are just a few key examples showing why understanding the context of each book is so important.

The first five books of the Bible were written by Moses roughly 3500 years ago, and some of the events he describes occurred many hundreds and even thousands of years prior to that. The setting is the ancient Near East and Egypt. And, because God, in His grace and kindness, always meets us right where we are and speaks in ways we can understand, He spoke to those people in those times in ways that were culturally relevant and understandable to them — even though it may seem strange to us.

It's important to know that books like the Psalms, Proverbs, Job, and Ecclesiastes are a special type of literature. They are songs, poems, and wisdom literature.

Many of the individual psalms, especially the psalms of David, are like short, self-contained stories. David may start a psalm (song) in the pits of despair and hopelessness. But by the time you get to the end of the psalm, he has rallied and is now confident in God and full of hope! So even though every verse of the Bible is inspired and perfect, you can't just quote a verse from the beginning of one of those psalms and expect to have the whole truth.

For example, David begins one psalm with these words:

> *How long, O LORD? Will You forget me forever? How long will You hide Your face from me?*
> (PSALM 13:1, NKJV)

That's not a verse you're likely to put on your refrigerator. What's more, the larger witness of the Bible is that God couldn't and wouldn't ever "forget" any of us. Nor does He hide His face from us. So, quoting that verse out of context is misleading. And by the time David gets to the final verse of his song, he writes:

> *I will sing to the LORD, because He has dealt bountifully with me.*
> (PSALM 13:6, NKJV)

Here's another example. When reading the prophetic books of the Old Testament, it's so very helpful to understand the historic context of when the prophecies were delivered, to whom, and why.

Also, when we get to the Gospels in the New Testament, it's vital to understand that Jesus came to fulfill three roles — all of which were prophesied in the Old Testament: Prophet, Priest, and King.

Sometimes in the Gospels, Jesus is speaking as the final "old covenant" prophet to that specific generation of Jewish people, and His words will only make sense in that context. (For more light on this, see Lens 3: "Read Your Bible With an Understanding of the Two Covenants.")

In Matthew 24 and Luke 17, Jesus points to the magnificent hilltop Second Temple in Jerusalem and tells His disciples that one day soon it will be utterly destroyed. He was delivering a specific prophetic message to a specific generation of people living in Israel. (By the way, Jesus' prophecy was fulfilled. Forty years after His crucifixion, almost to the day, Roman armies began surrounding Jerusalem to lay siege to it. Within a few months, that temple was a pile of rubble.)

It's instructive to do an in-depth search of the Gospels of Matthew and Luke for the term "this generation."

> There are so many prophetic things Jesus said that were specifically for the generation of people who were hearing His words at the moment He spoke them.

That doesn't mean, however, that those words don't have meaning for us today. As we've already seen, all Scripture is alive, and the Holy Spirit can use any verse at any time to speak a timely message to you.

Here's another example of reading in context. Much of your New Testament is made up of letters from the apostle Paul. All of his letters were written to specific churches or individuals between the years A.D. 40 and A.D. 66. Those churches and people were living in very specific cultures with very specific problems, needs, and mindsets.

The believers in Corinth who received the letters of First and Second Corinthians were facing a different set of challenges than the Christians Paul wrote to in Galatia (the letter to the Galatians). The cultural customs varied from city to city as well.

It's very helpful to know that when Paul wrote them, he often had two goals in mind. He wanted to help make sure they understood the doctrines and truths of the new Christian faith. But he also wrote to answer specific questions they had previously written to him. Or to address specific problems in the church that had been reported to him.

So, each of Paul's letters tends to have a *doctrinal* section and a *pastoral* section. People and churches sometimes get on shaky ground when they try to build doctrines or rules around things Paul addressed in a pastoral section of one of his letters.

For example, in First Corinthians, Paul, presumably in response to a question he'd received from them, writes:

> *Every man who prays or prophesies with his head covered dishonors his head. But every woman who prays or prophesies with her head uncovered dishonors her head — it is the same as having her head shaved. For if a woman does not cover her head, she might as well have her hair cut off; but if it is a disgrace for a woman to have her hair cut off or her head shaved, then she should cover her head.*
>
> (1 CORINTHIANS 11:4–6, NIV)

Throughout 20 centuries of church history, right down to our time, there have been a few Christian groups and denominations who chose to view Paul's words to the church at Corinth as "doctrine." As a result, those groups required women to have their heads covered during services while forbidding men to wear hats. Yet most churches in most times have viewed Paul's instructions as being very specific to that particular place, time, and culture.

Again, that doesn't mean the Holy Spirit won't use the New Testament's "pastoral" passages to speak truth, instruction, and correction to you.

Remember this...

Learning to read the Bible in context is "Lens #1" because it is a great place to begin. Once you know how to read your Bible in this way, you're better equipped to go on to other modes of reading the Scriptures.

Lens # 2

READ YOUR BIBLE

As a Redemption Story

Reframe it ...

Imagine you find an old, dusty book in the attic of your grandparents' house. Its pages are worn. Its leather cover cracked with age. It's heavy and holds the weight of countless stories. As you flip through the pages, you realize it's not any book — it's history, detailing trials, triumphs, and love.

The first chapters describe the foundation of your family. But as you read on, the narrative takes a turn. A mistake causes a rift, leading to pain and brokenness. The story becomes a journey to restore what was lost.

You come to a pivotal chapter where everything changes. A recent ancestor, someone much like a hero, steps forward with a plan to bring the family back together. This person, driven by love, undertakes great sacrifices. Their actions ripple through generations past, present, and future, altering the course of the story from despair to hope.

The family begins to heal. The final chapters, still being written, speak of restoration and unity, a testament to the power of love and redemption.

This book in your hands, with its tale of separation and reunion, mirrors the redemptive narrative of the Bible.

From the origin stories of Genesis to redemption through Jesus to His ultimate victory at the end of the book, Scripture invites us to see ourselves within its pages.

We can recognize how we're part of creation, a fall, and redemption from that fall. It's something personal yet universal. A story where love wins and where every lost son and daughter can come home.

Sometimes you have to "zoom out" to see the bigger picture. If you've used an online map service like Google Maps, you're familiar with this need. Someone mentions the name of a small town you've never heard of, so you decide to look it up to see where it is. But the first view that comes up is a "close-up" of the town. You see the grid of streets and that a river runs nearby. But you still have no idea where that town actually is.

So you "zoom out" a bit. At that point you see the names of other towns in the same area, but unless you recognize the name of one of those communities, you still have no idea where the mystery town is located. So you zoom out again. And you keep zooming out until you see the familiar outline of the state the town is in. You'll probably also see the familiar outlines of oceans or large lakes. Then and only then do you have a good sense of where that town is and how it relates to the rest of the world.

Your Bible is a lot like that. There are a lot of benefits to be had in studying a specific verse or chapter of the Bible. But your understanding and clarity will take a giant leap forward if you first "zoom out" to see the bigger, grander story your Bible is telling. It is a redemption story. You're about to discover what that means.

In the opening pages of Genesis, we find the seeds for everything that follows. The Bible presents us with a perfect world. Everything is in harmony, and humanity enjoys a rich, intimate, relaxed relationship with God. But this heaven on earth doesn't last. With Adam and Eve's decision to eat from the forbidden tree, everything changes. Sin enters the picture, and with it, death and separation from God. (See Genesis 3)

Romans 5:12-14 (TPT) says:

> *When Adam sinned, the entire world was affected. Sin entered human experience, and death was the result. And so death followed this sin, casting its shadow over all humanity, because all have sinned. Sin was in the world before Moses gave the written law, but it was not charged against them where no law existed. Yet death reigned as king from Adam to Moses even though they hadn't broken a command the way Adam had. The first man, Adam, was a picture of the Messiah, who was to come.*

From the point of Adam's rebellion forward, both creation and humanity became broken and hostages to darkness. This moment, often referred to as "the fall," is crucial because it explains why the world is the way it is today — filled with beauty and goodness but also riddled with suffering and evil. It explains the need for redemption and payment of ransom.

> And redemption requires a Redeemer.
> Payment of ransom requires a Payer.

As we move through the Old Testament, we find stories that, on the surface, might seem disconnected. However, when viewed through the lens of redemption, they are all little pieces of a larger, beautiful mosaic showing hope and mercy. They tell the story of a God working to restore the relationship lost in the fall.

Through laws, prophets, kings, and judges, God was continuously reaching out to humanity. Guiding them, keeping the promise of redemption alive.

The centerpiece of all the activity in the Old Testament is the creation of a "people." The call of Abraham, the 12 sons born to his grandson Jacob, and the eventual formation of those sons into 12 large "tribes" of descendants are all about the creation of that "people" — Israel.

That people had a purpose. A mission. It was to be the physical and spiritual carrier of that Redeemer who, when the time in history was just right, would emerge from them to become the Savior of the whole world.

All the scriptures, stories, prophecies, and laws are not just a random series of historical incidents but serve to lay the groundwork for the arrival of Jesus. We discover Him to be a "second and final Adam," who will succeed where the first Adam failed.

In this beautiful Isaiah 61:1 prophecy, the future "second Adam" describes His mission:

> "The Spirit of the Lord God is upon Me, because the Lord has anointed Me to preach good tidings to the poor; He has sent Me to heal the brokenhearted, to proclaim liberty to the captives, and the opening of the prison to those who are bound."
> (NKJV)

When we arrive at the Gospels, we find ourselves at the pivotal moment in this grand redemption story. Jesus enters the scene not just as a historical figure but as the fulfillment of all the Old Testament's promises and prophecies. Only in hindsight were the first Jewish Christians able to see that everything in the Old Testament had been pointing to Jesus all along.

- He was there in the animals God personally sacrificed in order to clothe shame-filled Adam and Eve after the fall (Genesis 3:21).

- He was there when God took Abraham's part in a covenant sacrifice ceremony while Abraham slept (Genesis 15:8-21).

- He was there as the substitute ram provided by God when Abraham was about to sacrifice his miracle son (Genesis 22:13).

- He was there as the sacrifice lamb in the Passover meal and the life-protecting blood on the doorposts on the evening before God delivered the 12 tribes of Israel from slavery in Egypt (Exodus 12:1-30).

- He was there in the red-colored thread or cord that Rahab hung in her window as a sign that she and everyone in her household should be spared (Joshua 2:1-22).

A thousand other examples could be mentioned, but you're getting the idea. By the way, that last example, Rahab and that red cord, have provided the name for this truth that Jesus is symbolized and foretold throughout the Old Testament. It's been called "The Scarlet Thread of Redemption." Of course, scarlet is the color of blood, and as you may have noticed in the handful of examples above, blood and sacrifice are a recurring theme.

A passage in the book of Hebrews talks about this very thing. In a section talking about Moses and how the rituals of the Tabernacle pointed to Jesus, the writer says, *"Actually, nearly everything under the law was purified with blood, since forgiveness only comes through an outpouring of blood"* (Hebrews 9:22, TPT).

This blood-red narrative thread woven through the Bible from Genesis to the Gospels reveal a lovely, cohesive story of redemption.

And it isn't only history; it's a living reality that continues today. Through Jesus, we are invited into the harmony of Eden, offered forgiveness for our sins, thoroughly cleansed and made whole, and given the guarantee of eternal life.

Remember this...

That's Redemption. Zoom out, and you'll find that the Bible is a story of a loving God seeking to heal and repair, through a second and final Adam, everything the first Adam had broken. The Old Testament is the account of God preparing to bring that second Adam (Jesus) into the world. The Gospels take place in the transition period. The rest of the New Testament explains what it means for you and me.

Lens #3

READ YOUR BIBLE

With an Understanding of the Two Covenants

Reframe it ...

Even if you knew nothing about the Bible and just picked one up, the Table of Contents would give you a big hint as to its structure. There's a reason the books of your Bible are divided into two groups: the Old Testament and the New Testament. (By the way, the word *testament* as used here means "covenant," which in turn means a sacred, legally binding agreement. Think, "holy contract.")

> **The 39 books of the Old Testament made up the sacred Scriptures for Israelites and Jews for centuries.**

By the time Jesus arrived on the scene, those 39 books were often divided into three sections and referred to as: (1) the Law; (2) the Prophets; and (3) the Psalms.

Jesus referenced all three of these groups in a conversation with His disciples shortly after His resurrection. Jesus' arrest, torture, and death had confused His followers. Even though He'd repeatedly told them it was going to happen, along with His resurrection, they still hadn't seen it coming. So, while Jesus shared a meal with them . . .

> *He said to them, "These are my words that I spoke to you while I was still with you, that everything written about me in **the Law** of Moses and **the Prophets** and **the Psalms** must be fulfilled."*
>
> (LUKE 24:44, ESV, EMPHASIS ADDED)

There they are — the three types of Old Testament books! Here, Jesus is giving us a major clue as to how to read the Old Testament. As He suggests here and as other scriptures confirm, much of the Old Testament was actually pointing to Jesus all along. It's just that the Israelites didn't have eyes to see it yet.

We'll talk more about this in the next "lens," but for now, just know that when you're reading the Old Testament, you're reading about events and rituals that point to something. Actually, they're pointing toward some*one*. That someone is Jesus and what He was sent to accomplish for us.

The final structure of the Bible shouts that God's plan for restoring mankind back to intimate connection and relationship with Himself had two phases.

"Phase 1" unfolds in the Old Testament. And from the very first chapter of Genesis to the final lines of Malachi, *covenant* and covenantal language are all over the place. "Phase 2" begins with Jesus' victory over sin and death and His ascension to the right hand of God in heaven. The three-year ministry of Jesus serves as a sort of transitional time between Phase 1 and Phase 2.

God has chosen to work through covenant arrangements. We can speculate about *why* this is, but it's obvious that it's true. As we noted above, a covenant is a solemn, sacred contract, agreement, or treaty between two persons or two parties. And it's clear from reading the Bible that God, even though He is *GOD*, willingly chooses to bind Himself to certain agreements with us mere humans.

Here's the thing:

> **God — because He is good and holy and just — always keeps His side of an agreement.**

He cannot lie. He will never cheat. And He always does what He says He will do. In other words, He's the ideal Person to be in an agreement with.

Reading through Genesis, we see that God made covenants with Adam and Eve, (which they broke). He made a covenant with Noah and his descendants, (which they quickly forgot). And He made a covenant with Abraham. And that covenant contained two promises.

One was that, although Abraham was old and childless, he would have descendants who would become a vast nation of people. The second was that, out of that nation of people, a Savior-Messiah would emerge. And through Him, all the nations of the earth would be blessed (Genesis 22:18).

But the big covenant (or testament), the one that gives the "Old Testament" its name, is the covenant God made with the Israelites through Moses. That's why it's often called the "Mosaic Covenant." The books of Exodus, Leviticus, Numbers, and Deuteronomy — four out of the first five books of the Bible — are all about how God used Moses to mediate and deliver a covenant agreement between God and the 12 tribes of Israel.

In fulfillment of that first promise made to Abraham, the Mosaic covenant turned 12 related tribes of people descended from Abraham's 12 grandsons into a nation. A covenant people. A "chosen" people. But *chosen* for what, exactly? To answer that question, we have to "zoom out" a bit. And it involves that second promise made to Abraham. The one about that Savior-Messiah.

In the previous chapter, "Lens 2: Read Your Bible as a Redemption Story," we saw that as soon as mankind fell — breaking humanity and creation itself and cutting us off from intimate connection to Him — God set a plan in motion to repair what sin had broken and to restore what had been lost.

That plan involved getting a Savior or Redeemer into the world. We now know, in hindsight, that this Redeemer would need to be fully human yet fully God. One of us. In that way, He would be another "Adam," yet this second Adam would not sin like the first one did. We know Him as Jesus Christ (literally, Jesus the Messiah).

The whole Old Testament can be viewed as the story of God's preparations and covenantal prerequisites for getting Jesus into the Earth so the process of fixing what had been broken could begin.

It's all pointing to Him.

And it's all about God moving heaven and earth to get Jesus — God in human flesh — delivered to us so He could make things right.

There are lots of little clues in the Old Testament that the old covenant wasn't the final phase of God's plan. But in Jeremiah chapter 31, we find not a "clue" but an explicit announcement:

> "Behold, the days are coming, declares the Lord, when I will make **a new covenant** with the house of Israel and the house of Judah, **not like the covenant that I made with their fathers** on the day when I took them by the hand to bring them out of the land of Egypt, my covenant that they broke, though I was their husband, declares the Lord."
>
> (JEREMIAH 31:31–32, ESV, EMPHASIS ADDED)

Highlighted in bold in those verses are two important points. The first is that a "new covenant" is coming for the Israelite people at some point. Other Old Testament prophecies make it clear that this "new" covenant will not *just* be for "the house of Israel and the house of Judah." They indicate that when that new covenant came, it would make connection to God through covenant available to the gentiles, too. (See, for example, Isaiah 56:6-7)

The other key detail is that this "new" covenant would be a different kind of covenant than the first one. As the prophecy said, it will be "not like the covenant" that God made through Moses.

But that raises the question: "Different in what way?"

Our gracious God always deals with us in ways we can understand. In other words, He meets us where we are and speaks our language.

For people living in the times in which the Bible was written, one thing they understood very well was the concept of covenant. In fact, there were two main *kinds* of covenants back then.

One was the kind of solemn, unbreakable agreement two leaders of relatively equal strength would make. This is sometimes called a "Parity Covenant" because it was a treaty between two kings or tribal heads of relatively equal power and status.

This is a covenant in which two leaders or kings come together and pledge loyalty to one another. Each says to the other something along these lines: "If you are attacked, I'll consider that an attack on me and come to your defense. If you have a need, I'll supply it if I can. What is mine is yours. We are now family."

Again, this kind of covenant made two separate families or peoples "one." The ceremony also sometimes included cutting one or more animals in half. The two parties would walk between the halved animal carcasses while swearing, "May this or worse happen to me if I ever violate my faithfulness to this covenant."

Such a covenant was usually sealed with a symbolic exchange of items — often rings and/or robes — and culminated with a meal. As you can now see, another good name for a Parity Covenant would be Equal-to-Equal. (By the way, there are a lot of parallels between this kind of covenant and the Christian marriage covenant.)

We now know, in hindsight, that this is the kind of covenant God wanted to make with mankind all along. But there was one problem. Do you see the hang-up?

Where could God find an "equal" to represent humanity in a Parity Covenant agreement? Where could there possibly be a fully human, "one-of-us" person who could handle our side of the arrangement?

There wasn't one! Which explains why God had a two-phase plan. That's where that other kind of covenant comes in.

In the ancient world of the Bible, there was a kind of covenant historians now call a Suzerain-Vassal Treaty. *Suzerain* means "boss, lord, or master." And vassal means servant. So, another way to label such an arrangement would be a Master-Servant covenant.

In ancient times, a very powerful king who was in a position to dominate neighboring nations would sometimes enter into a Suzerain-Vassal treaty with those weaker kings. Such a king might go to his weak little neighbor-king and say something like:

> "Hey, we both know I'm much stronger and bigger than you. I could crush you and take over your country if I wanted to. But here's a much better option for both of us: Let's both sign an agreement in which you swear you'll be loyal to me and pay me an annual tax (tribute). In return, I'll protect you if you're attacked. Of course, if you refuse to sign this treaty, I'll probably just go ahead and destroy you. Which option do you choose?"

These kinds of treaties were very common in the ancient lands of the Bible. Archeologists have dug up countless clay tablets that contain the written records of Suzerain-Vassal treaties between two kings. The Old Testament mentions this kind of arrangement in numerous places. See 2 Kings 17:3 and 24:1, for example.

The terms of these Suzerain-Vassal covenants were always spelled out in detail in treaty documents that had a common structure. Keep that in mind. Now you know the two most common kinds of covenants that people in the time in which Moses lived were familiar with.

Again, God always chooses to operate through covenant.

He, in His kindness, always deals with us in ways we can understand. And so, when the time came to begin unfolding His plan to fix what had been broken in the fall, it made sense that He would use a kind of covenant familiar to the people He was going to have a covenant relationship with. But as we've already seen, the only kind of covenant available to God in this period of time was the Suzerain-Vassal form.

Moses, having grown up as a prince of Egypt, would have been very familiar with this type of treaty. Egypt, as a "superpower" in that era, had lots of *vassal* nations, which it dominated as *suzerain* (or lord). So, God spoke to Moses from a burning bush about leading the 12 Israelite tribes out of Egypt.

Then, after the "exodus" from Egypt, God met with Moses — the God-chosen leader of Israel's millions — on the top of Mount Sinai. There, God offered to enter into a covenant agreement with Israel.

The core of that covenant was the Ten Commandments. But the expanded version of the agreement is spelled out in the Old Testament books of Leviticus and Deuteronomy. We call it the "Mosaic covenant" because Moses was the mediator or representative dealing with God on behalf of the Israelites.

Over the centuries, hundreds of theologians and students of ancient history have pointed out that the structure of the Mosaic covenant in Exodus and Deuteronomy closely parallels the structure of other Suzerian-Vassal treaties from that time period.

God was offering to be Israel's *Suzerain* (albeit a kind, patient, and benevolent one) and to let them be His one and only *vassal* nation on earth. He would be their Lord and they would be His loyal servants. There is one very important thing to know about this kind of covenant.

One important aspect of all Suzerain-Vassal treaties, including the Mosaic covenant, is that they're *conditional*. A suzerain would issue a list of requirements or conditions or "stipulations" the vassal was required to follow.

If and only *if* the vassal kept these conditions, *then* the suzerain would provide the promised benefits and protections. If the vassal didn't meet the conditions, the suzerain was no longer legally (covenantally) obligated to fulfill those promises.

> **In other words, this kind of covenant is a conditional,**
> **IF/THEN agreement. *If* you obey, then you will be blessed.**
> **If . . . then.**

It's no accident that we see this If/Then language all over the Old Testament. Look at the often quoted 2 Chronicles 7:14 for example:

> "***If*** *My people who are called by My name will humble themselves, and pray and seek My face, and turn from their wicked ways,* **then** *I will hear from heaven, and will forgive their sin and heal their land."*
> (NKJV, EMPHASIS ADDED)

If . . . then. We see it over and over in the Old Testament scriptures. Why? Because the Mosaic covenant is a conditional covenant, and if you've read much of the Old Testament, you already know that those Israelite tribes were constantly failing to live up to their side of the agreement.

Here's the good news: That covenant was never intended to be the "end game" in God's plan to rescue mankind. The old covenant was always just a necessary stepping stone to something "new" and "better."

Its only job was to keep a people — the Jewish people — intact long enough to get Jesus the Messiah into the world. We've already noted that God clearly announced to the old covenant people through Jeremiah that a "new" covenant was coming someday.

We've also seen that the promised new covenant wouldn't just be "new," but would also be a different *kind* of covenant. What kind?

A Parity Covenant in which mankind had a representative who could actually make a peer-to-peer covenant with the God of the Universe.

> Only "God the Son," in human flesh, could enter into a Parity Covenant with "God the Father." And He did.

The old covenant served its purpose well, but when the new one came, the old one became obsolete and passed away. So says Hebrews chapter eight:

> *But now Jesus the Messiah has accepted a priestly ministry which far surpasses theirs* [*that of the priests of the Mosaic covenant*]*, since he is the catalyst of* **a better covenant which contains far more wonderful promises!** *For if that first covenant had been faultless no one would have needed a second one to* **replace** *it. But God revealed the defect and limitation of the first . . . This proves that by establishing this new covenant* **the first is now obsolete, ready to expire, and about to disappear.**
> (vv. 6–8, 13, TPT)

Do you see it? The New made the Old "obsolete." And at the time of the writing of Hebrews, it was already "ready to expire" and "about to disappear."

Not only did that passage in Hebrews declare the old covenant "obsolete," it also said the new one is "better" and built on "more wonderful promises." In what other ways is the new better than the old?

The biggest reason is that it isn't a Suzerain-Vassal covenant. No, as we've seen, it's a Parity Covenant between God the Father and God the Son. But that presents this question: How do we get in on it?

The answer is we participate by being *in* Jesus. Many New Testament scriptures talk about how the miracle of the new birth — that is, being born again — is a process that puts us "in Christ" and Him in us.

Just look at these verses for examples: Romans 6:3; Romans 8:1; 1 Corinthians 1:30; 2 Corinthians 5:17; Galatians 2:20; Galatians 3:27; Ephesians 1:3–14; and many others.

Keep in mind the nature of a Parity Covenant. In this case, God the Son (Jesus) stands face-to-face with God the Father as they pledge covenant faithfulness to one another. By being "baptized into Christ" (Galatians 3:27), we are "in Him." Through Christ we gain complete and full access to God the Father.

> **Instead of getting what *we* deserve,
> we get what Jesus qualifies for.**

Do you think Jesus will ever be unfaithful to His covenant with the Father? Do you think He will ever fail to hold up His end of the agreement? Of course not!

This puts the familiar verse 2 Corinthians 1.20 in a fresh light:

> *For no matter how many promises God has made, they are "Yes"* **in Christ**. *And so* **through him** [**Christ**] *the "Amen" is spoken* **by us** *to the glory of God.*
> (NIV, EMPHASIS ADDED)

Do you see it? This is not a conditional Suzerain-Vassal covenant like the old covenant. Jesus has met and continues to meet any and all conditions for walking in the promises of God. No wonder they call the gospel "good news."

In closing, here is a quick comparison between the old and the new covenants:

	Old Covenant	New Covenant
Mediator	Moses	Jesus
Promises	Conditional	Unconditional "in Christ"
Access	One nation only (Israel)	All Believing Israel and All Believing Gentiles
Sacrifice for Sin	Annual	Once for All Time
Access to God	Limited and Remote; Priests in the Middle	Direct and Intimate; Because We Come to God "Through Christ"

Remember this...

Now you know. When you read the Old Testament, you're reading an account of a people in a covenant that is different from the one it is our privilege to participate in . . . "in Christ." Understanding this will keep you from getting confused about whether the promises of God belong to you or not.

So how should new covenant people read the scriptures of the old covenant? That is the topic for the next "lens."

Lens #4

READ YOUR BIBLE

Through a "New Covenant" Lens

Reframe it ...

As mentioned in the Introduction, most of us were handed a Bible when we became Christians, or even before we made the decision to follow Christ, and were exhorted to read it. Yet one of the most confusing and often unhelpful things any believer can do is try to read the Old Testament without the correct understanding of how the old covenant is different from the new covenant.

Hopefully, the previous section provided you with a great start on just such an understanding. Now you know God's dealings with Israel in the Old Testament period were founded on the Suzerain-Vassal form of covenant. We also saw that this wasn't the kind of covenant God preferred to use, but it was the only kind available to Him until He could get Jesus into the world.

The restrictive nature of Suzerain-Vassal covenants results in many Old Testament passages in which the Mosaic Law seems harsh and even cruel. For example, Deuteronomy 21:18–21 seems to suggest that chronically rebellious children should be tried before the elders of the city and, if found guilty, be stoned to death.

We also see harsh punishments for idolatry, witchcraft, and various other violations of the old covenant stipulations. And then there are the passages in which Israel's armies are commanded to wipe out populations of entire cities.

What are we to do with that? How do we reconcile that with John 3:16's declaration, straight from Jesus' own mouth . . .

> *"For God so loved the world that He gave His only begotten Son, that whoever believes in Him should not perish but have everlasting life."* (NKJV)

It's important to keep in mind that the entire purpose of the old covenant was to create a people who could remain free enough from the corrupting, defiling impacts of pagan idolatry long enough to get Jesus into the world.

If God didn't accomplish that, all of mankind was doomed. Read the Old Testament itself as a drama playing out across several thousand years in which God's enemy tries, in vain, to stop God's redemptive plan. Put another way, the whole Old Testament can be viewed as the story of God working in history to put in place all that was legally necessary for the arrival of Jesus, alongside Satan's futile efforts to stop God's grand rescue plan from coming to pass.

Note the phrase "legally necessary" in the paragraph above. Too few Christians understand that God built the universe upon a legal and judicial framework. Once God legally granted dominion and stewardship of Earth to mankind (Genesis 1:26–28), He was constrained by His own righteousness and holiness to operate within the judicial rules He had established.

> In other words, although a sovereign God theoretically could have cheated at the game He invented, His character would never allow Him to do so.

This meant that if God was going to fulfill His promise to get our Savior into the Earth, He would have to do so "legally." And as we saw in the previous "Lens" chapter, the best covenant available to God in the Old Testament era was the rigid Suzerain-Vassal covenant, which was basically a Master-Servant arrangement. So, God — being righteous and good and just and holy — operated perfectly within the conditional "rules" of that kind of covenant.

But His plan all along was to get another kind of covenant in place. The kind of covenant that would make us — both Jews and gentiles — not *servants* but rather *sons* and *daughters*. But as we've seen, putting that covenant in place meant that before He could be a Father, He'd have to be a Master for a season.

In the Old Testament, everything that came after the fall of man seemingly depicts a cosmic chess match between God and His crafty but inferior enemy.

If the Old Testament narrative sometimes seems harsh and hard, it is only because the stakes of that battle were so very high.

The eternal fate of humanity and control of planet Earth literally hung in the balance. Yet, move by move, God brilliantly advanced His plan.

First, He called a man (Abram) — one willing to sacrifice his own son in faith. That man would produce a people (Israel) whose intricately prescribed sacrificial system of worship would, by judicial necessity, model and forerun the ultimate solution to the crisis Adam caused.

The blood-soaked Old Testament is the war chronicle of the battle to get Jesus, the "Second and Final Adam," to Earth so He could make us beloved sons and daughters of God. Every detail of every incident speaks of Him. Points to Him. Prepares for Him.

This is the key to reading the Old Testament with a new covenant lens. Yes, there is great value in reading the Old Testament, but it must be read with an understanding that the people in it were operating under a different kind of covenant. And it must be read understanding that the battle to preserve Israel as the carrier of the future Savior of the world was raging throughout those centuries.

Read with the understanding that God was flawlessly and faithfully doing what was necessary to rescue us all. But that He couldn't fully be all He wanted to be for, in, and to us until He got the new covenant in place.

Finally, it's confusing and ultimately destructive to try to drag aspects of the Law of Moses — the old covenant — into the grace-filled blessings of the new covenant. The New Covenant's "law of love," in action, causes us to fulfill the spirit of all the Old Covenant laws anyway.

The entire book of Hebrews is basically an explanation of why the new covenant is superior to the old covenant and why the old was no longer needed once the new one was in place. We looked at a few verses from Hebrews chapter eight in the previous sections. Here are verses six and seven from that same chapter.

> But now Jesus, our High Priest, has been given a ministry that is far superior to the old priesthood, for he is the one who mediates for us a far better covenant with God, based on better promises. **If the first covenant had been faultless, there would have been no need for a second covenant to replace it.**
> (NLT, EMPHASIS ADDED)

Notice that, according to that last verse, the first covenant had flaws and that the "second covenant" replaced it. The writer of that chapter, in verses 8–12, then goes on to quote the full prophecy from Jeremiah in which the prophet reveals that a new covenant is coming *"with the house of Israel and with the house of Judah"* (Hebrews 8:8, NKJV).

The chapter closes with this verse that we examined in the previous section:

When God speaks of a "new" covenant, it means he has made the first one obsolete. It is now out of date and will soon disappear (Hebrews 8:13, NLT).

It's inappropriate to try to mix the rules of the old with the new. Jesus had this in mind when He told the Pharisees that you can't put new wine in an old wineskin (Matthew 9:17). We can't read the "conditional" promises of the Old Testament as if it is still on us to meet those conditions.

> **Jesus became — once and for all time — our Conditions Meeter. Jesus was and is the fulfilment of the Mosaic Law.**

This is the meaning of Jesus' mysterious and often-misunderstood comment to the Pharisees: *"Do not think that I have come to abolish the Law or the Prophets; I have not come to abolish them but to fulfill them"* (Matthew 5:17, NIV). Jesus fulfilled every single requirement of that Law on your behalf. He has met all the conditions of the Old Testament's conditional promises for us . . . and bore the consequences of our disobedience on the Cross!

Remember this...

There is great encouragement and blessing in seeing all the ways the old pointed to Jesus in the new. So, when you read the Old Testament, be looking for Jesus! And also be looking with gratitude and wonder and the battle that took place to get Him into the world so He could do the redemptive work and make the "new" and "better" covenant we enjoy possible.

Lens #5

READ YOUR BIBLE

As a Treasure Chest of Revealed Mysteries

Reframe it ...

Mystery novels and movies are one of the most popular genres year after year. It seems everyone loves a good mystery.

Imagine discovering an old, worn map in a dusty attic, hinting at hidden treasure. This map doesn't lead to a chest of gold buried under an X on some distant island. Rather, it guides you on a journey of discovery. Through texts overflowing with mysteries waiting to be uncovered.

Each story, parable, and letter in the Bible is like that — treasures waiting to be found. And they aren't hidden away for a select few. They are there for all who approach the Bible with an open heart.

Reading the Bible as a treasure chest means seeing beyond the surface. It involves digging deeper. It means exploring with excitement and expectancy. It means anticipating the finding of rich wisdom and liberating truth.

This approach transforms your interaction with the Bible from routine reading to thrilling exploration.

One in which every turn of the page presents new insights and life-giving revelations.

The New Testament mentions the word "mystery" quite a bit — especially the letters of Paul. Whenever you see the word mystery in the New Testament, the Greek word *musterion* is usually beneath it. And that Greek word has a slightly different meaning from the one we usually associate with "mystery."

Musterion refers to something that was previously hidden but has now been revealed. In other words, a better translation for *musterion* might be "revealed secret."

Mysteries, in the biblical context, are not puzzles designed for entertainment but truths unveiled by the Holy Spirit — by revelation. (Please note that the word *reveal* lies at the root of "revelation.") These mysteries are divine strategies and truths, laid from the foundation of the world, now made known to us. They invite us into a deeper understanding of God's character, His kingdom, and His purposes for humanity.

Central to the treasure chest of the Bible is "THE mystery," as Paul often refers to it — the profound revealing of Jesus Christ.

> *... the mystery which has been hidden from ages and from generations, but now has been revealed to His saints. To them God willed to make known what are the riches of the glory of this mystery among the Gentiles: which is Christ in you, the hope of glory.*
> (COLOSSIANS 1:26–27, NKJV)

This mystery is nothing less than the incarnation of God Himself, the bringing together of heaven and Earth, and the reconciliation of humanity with the Divine through the cross. God had this in mind from the very beginning, but no one saw it coming. The old covenant scholars studied the Hebrew Scriptures endlessly. They knew a Messiah was coming. But the Messiah's true mission was nothing like what they expected.

God's plan to restore with a "Second and Final Adam" what the first Adam had broken had to remain a secret — a mystery — until the time arrived to execute that plan. Not only did the Jewish experts in the Old Testament not see it coming, Satan and his hierarchy of demonic entities didn't see it coming either. That's exactly why Paul wrote:

> *No, the wisdom we speak of is* **the mystery of God** *— his plan that was previously hidden, even though he made it for our ultimate glory before the world began. But the rulers of this world have not understood it;* ***if they had, they would not have crucified our glorious Lord.***
>
> (1 CORINTHIANS 2:7–8, NLT, EMPHASIS ADDED)

But that big, overarching "mystery" is not the only one revealed in your Bible. Jesus' parables and a significant portion of the four Gospels of Matthew, Mark, Luke, and John serve as windows into the mysteries of the kingdom of God. These stories, while simple on the surface, contain depths of wisdom and revelation.

They invite listeners to perceive the invisible realities of God's kingdom, where the last are first, the humble are exalted, and seemingly insignificant acts of faith can move mountains.

Each parable, each teaching of Jesus, is a gem within the treasure chest. Each offers insights into living in harmony with God's will and experiencing the fullness of life He offers. Each reveals the nature of God's love, the value of forgiveness, and the power of faith.

Furthermore, diving into the wisdom books of the Bible — Proverbs, Ecclesiastes, and Job — is a step deeper into ancient mines of knowledge and insight. These books are not merely collections of old sayings but maps to mystery. Within their chapters lie the keys to understanding human nature, the pursuit of a meaningful life, and the complexity of the world around us. They challenge us to think, reflect, and grow in light of God's truth.

Proverbs 3:5-6 notably instructs us, *"Trust in the LORD with all your heart, and lean not on your own understanding; in all your ways acknowledge Him, and He shall direct your paths"* (NKJV).

The Bible, in its entirety, addresses the deepest mysteries of life and faith. From the philosophical questions of Job to the poetic musings of the Psalms, from history to wisdom literature to prophecy to the apocalyptic visions of Revelation. Scripture explores the breadth of human experience with honesty and depth. It offers solace in suffering, wisdom in confusion, and hope in despair.

As we engage with these texts, we find the Bible encourages us to bring our questions, doubts, and fears before God, confident He will provide understanding.

For thousands of years, people have wondered, "Why am I here? What is my purpose in life?" And big, universal questions like, "Why does the world seem broken?" or, "Why are people capable of such evil?" and, "If God is good, why is there so much suffering and heartache in the world?

In the Bible, if you read with the right lenses, you'll find the answers to the deepest questions of life. Including answers about your identity, purpose, and destiny.

You'll discover your value in the eyes of our Creator and your place in the grand narrative He is unfolding.

Do you struggle with anxiety? Find peace in Philippians 4:6–7, which encourages you not to be anxious about anything, but in every situation, by prayer and petition, with thanksgiving, present your requests to God. So that the peace of God, which transcends all understanding, will guard your heart and mind in Christ Jesus.

Are you facing uncertainty about the future? Draw hope from Jeremiah 29:11, where God promises plans for prosperity and not disaster, to give you a future filled with hope.

Do you give into thoughts of insecurity? Remember that you are God's handiwork, created in Christ Jesus to do good works, which God prepared in advance for you to do (Ephesians 2:10).

Feeling overwhelmed by temptation? Find strength in 1 Corinthians 10:13, which assures you no temptation has overtaken you except what is common to mankind. And God is faithful; He will not let you be tempted beyond what you can bear.

Struggling with loss or mourning? Seek comfort in Matthew 5:4, *"Blessed are those who mourn, for they will be comforted"* (NIV).

Battling with anger or resentment? Look to Ephesians 4:31–32, which advises putting away all bitterness, rage, and anger and to be kind and compassionate to one another, forgiving each other, just as in Christ God forgave you.

Do you feel unloved or unworthy? Embrace the truth of Romans 8:38–39, which declares that nothing can separate you from the love of God that is in Christ Jesus our Lord, not even your fears for today or worries about tomorrow.

Facing financial difficulties? Philippians 4:19 offers assurance God will meet all your needs according to the riches of His glory in Christ Jesus.

Struggling with decision-making? James 1:5 encourages asking God, who gives generously to all without finding fault, for wisdom.

Dealing with loneliness or isolation? Hebrews 13:5 reminds us God has said, *"Never will I leave you; never will I forsake you"* (NIV).

As we explore the treasure chest of the Bible, we are invited to apply its wisdom to our lives — to let its truths transform us from the inside out. This process of transformation is both personal and communal, affecting not only our own lives but also influencing those around us. By living out the mysteries revealed in Scripture, we become beacons of light in a world searching for truth and meaning.

Remember this...

As you continue to explore the Bible, let it be with a heart open to the mysteries your heavenly Father has revealed on its pages. Let His Word be a lamp to your feet and a light to your path.

Yes, everyone loves a mystery story. And you could spend multiple lifetimes discovering the revealed mysteries embedded in the greatest story ever told.

Lens #6

READ YOUR BIBLE

As a Son, Not a Servant

Reframe it ...

In Lens #3: "Read Your Bible With an Understanding of the Two Covenants," you discovered the New Testament's "new covenant" was a very different kind of covenant than the Old Testament's "old covenant."

We saw that while the old one, by definition, made people servants or slaves of God, the new one made us family members of God by putting us "in" His Son, Jesus.

Now don't in any way dismiss the old covenant because it created "servants" of God. In its time, it was far, far better to be a slave to a kind, benevolent, gracious Master like God than the alternative. Namely, being a slave to Satan, who hates mankind with a vicious hatred. The old covenant was the best thing going — right up to the moment Jesus came along and made the new covenant possible.

From that day forward, the old covenant became, as the book of Hebrews tells us: flawed, inferior, and obsolete by comparison (Hebrews 8:6–13). This is why a "servant" mindset was appropriate for those under the old covenant. It was true to the nature of that covenant. But, in contrast, the new covenant creates sons and daughters of God.

Jesus scandalized the Pharisees and other Jewish religious leaders of His day by consistently referring to God as *"My Father."* He shocked them even further when He taught His disciples to pray, *"Our Father in heaven . . ."* (Matthew 6:9, NKJV).

This was a foretaste of what He was going to make possible through His death and resurrection. Right there in the opening lines of John's Gospel, we find these words concerning Jesus:

> But those who embraced him and took hold of his name he gave authority to become the children of God!
> (JOHN 1:12, TPT)

Paul understood this truth at a deep level. He had it in mind when he wrote:

> Yet all of this was so that [Jesus] would redeem and set free those held hostage to the law so that we would receive our freedom and a full legal adoption as his children. And so that we would know that we are his true children, God released the Spirit of Sonship into our hearts — moving us to cry out intimately, "My Father! My true Father!" Now we're no longer living like slaves under the law, but we enjoy being God's very own sons and daughters! And because we're his, we can access everything our Father has — for we are heirs because of what God has done!
> (GALATIANS 4:5–7, TPT)

Please understand that we use the term "son" and "sonship" in the generic sense in this section. In Christ there is neither male nor female, for we are all one in Christ (Galatians 3:28). That spirit of adoption that causes our born-again spirits to cry out "Father!" is present in both men and women. We become sons and daughters of God.

The apostle John declares this in his letter as well:

> *Dear friends, we are already God's children, but he has not yet shown us what we will be like when Christ appears. But we do know that we will be like him, for we will see him as he really is.*
> (1 JOHN 3:2, NLT)

Paul wrote the entire book of Galatians to correct people who were getting confused about which covenant they were living under. Some people had come in and taught the members of that church that they should start obeying certain parts of the old covenant rules and regulations.

Galatians is Paul sternly and forcefully reminding them that they were no longer servants or slaves under the old. That they, instead, were beloved children of God under the new.

> *So Christ has truly set us free. Now make sure that you stay free, and don't get tied up again in slavery to the law.*
> (GALATIANS 5:1, NLT)

In the parable of the prodigal son (Luke 15:11–32), Jesus presents two sons, neither of whom understood their true standing with their father. The wayward son, upon his return home, was prepared to be just another one of his father's servants. He thought he had forfeited his right to the privileges and blessings of sonship. But he was wrong.

Jesus, the storyteller, has the father welcoming the boy home and putting a signet ring on his finger and a robe of honor around his shoulders. Both of these items symbolize sonship. The boy thought his mistakes disqualified him from sonship. But he was wrong. He came with a slave mentality, but the father corrected it.

The other son in the story had a servant mentality as well. He complained to the father that he had "served him" his whole life and never disobeyed any commands yet had never been rewarded (Luke 15:29). In Jesus' telling of the story, the father's response to the son is, *"Son, you are always with me, and all that is mine is yours"* (v. 31, ESV).

Remember this...

From a distance, sons and servants sometimes look similar and seem to be doing similar things. Both are busy doing the Father's business. But there is a world of difference in terms of heart posture, access to the Father's presence, and receiving the Father's resources.

At the end of the day, servants go eat in the servants' quarters. And sons and daughters recline at the Father's table.

It is easy to adopt one of these two mindsets and then carry them into our reading of the Bible. Reading the Bible with a servant mindset puts you in the place of one or both of those two sons in Jesus' story. Trying to earn and merit and deserve instead of just gratefully receiving all that belongs to us because we are "in Jesus."

Lens #7

READ YOUR BIBLE

At The Right "Tree"

Reframe it ...

If you've read the first three chapters of your Bible, you know there were two special trees in the garden of Eden into which God placed the first human couple. There was a "Tree of Life," which seems to not only have been a source of eternal life but also the primary meeting spot for God to connect with His beloved Adam and Eve.

The other was the forbidden one — the Tree of Knowledge of Good and Evil. This one they had been ordered to stay away from. We won't take the time here to explore the reasons why God would even put a tree within reach if touching it would bring about terrible consequences. But it has to do with God's gift of free will — the power to choose.

> So, why did God give humanity free will? Because without choice there can be no such thing as real love.

Love *is* a choice. And at the heart of God's motivation for making this gorgeous world and placing humanity in it lies His desire to love and be loved.

Those opening chapters of Genesis reveal that the first humans exercised that precious gift of free will and ate of that forbidden tree. Doing so brought a curse upon themselves and upon the whole world. From that point forward, people were broken, and nature was broken.

Again, we call that "the fall," and what a fall it was. But almost immediately, God set a plan in place to repair all that had been broken. And as we saw in Lens 3: "Read Your Bible With an Understanding of the Two Covenants," the key to that plan was getting Jesus to the Earth.

It's all a bit shrouded in mystery, but there was clearly something about that *wrong* tree that caused our ancestral parents to be filled with shame, condemnation, and guilt. It made them *self*-conscious. And the worst effect of all — that shame, guilt, and self-consciousness — made them shrink back from enjoying the very thing they were created for. That is, enjoying God's love and fellowship — His presence. And from that moment onward, death reigned over humanity.

The fig leaves Adam and Eve sewed together were the first of a billion religious things mankind has frantically come up with to try to cover that shame and assuage that guilt. Tragically, at that other tree, self-conscious rule-following, which could only bring more death, instantly replaced enjoying God's presence, which is the only thing that can impart life.

Figuratively speaking, one big narrative of your Bible as a whole is that Jesus died at the Tree of Knowledge of Good and Evil (the cross) to give us a way back to the Tree of Life — the place where we meet and partner with God.

- Because of what Jesus accomplished through His death and resurrection, the terrible effects of the fall have been undone for all who are willing to believe it and receive it (Galatians 3:13).

- The hold of death was broken, and instead we received eternal life (1 Corinthians 15:55).

- Jesus died our spiritual death so we could have His supernatural everlasting life (1 John 5:11).

- Jesus also bore our shame (Hebrews 12:2).

- He bore our guilt (Hebrews 10:10–12).

- There is now no condemnation for those who are in Jesus (Romans 8:1).

And because, with the free gift of salvation, we also receive the gift of Jesus' own righteousness (2 Corinthians 5:21), we no longer need to shrink back from or avoid God's life-giving presence. As the author of Hebrews wrote:

> *So now we draw near freely and boldly to where grace is enthroned, to receive mercy's kiss and discover the grace we urgently need to strengthen us in our time of weakness.*
> (HEBREWS 4:16, TPT)

In other words, Jesus not only nullified the horrific effects of the Tree of Knowledge of Good and Evil, He opened the way back to the Tree of Life, where we belong. But here's the problem . . .

We are all saved at the Tree of Life. Yet, for too many Christians, after salvation, they were immediately taken by the hand and led back over to that other tree.

The tree where shame, guilt, self-consciousness, and futile, desperate religious rule-following fill our lives.

It's possible to read your Bible at either "tree." When you read the Bible in the light of the Tree of Life, you're reading it to hear the voice of your heavenly Father. You read it to "see" Jesus. You read it because the "living and active" words of God are life to your spirit, refreshment to your soul, and even healing to your body.

There, you read it using the other "lenses" you're discovering in this guide. And as you do, you are changed, almost effortlessly, from the inside out. When you hang out at the Tree of Life with your heavenly

Father, you are transformed from glory to glory (2 Corinthians 3:18). Whereas that other tree is where we become slaves to *self*-consciousness, at the Tree of Life we are liberated from the tyranny of self, and our focus moves to Jesus.

But most Christians are taught to read their Bibles in the light of that *other* tree. Because it is the tree where shame, guilt, and *self*-consciousness live, we open the Bible's pages to see where we've been messing up. We read to learn how far we're falling short of who we are supposed to be. We scan the pages for rules to follow and to add to an impossible, ever-growing list of *oughts* — that is, religious works and activities we should be doing.

At the Tree of Knowledge of Good and Evil, even reading the Bible becomes one of those *oughts*. Instead of an exciting appointment with the voice and heart of God, "Bible study" becomes a joyless, lifeless drudgery. A box to be checked, and nothing more.

In Jesus' day, the land of Israel was filled with people who had been reading the Scriptures at the wrong tree. The Pharisees, the Sadducees, and the Scribes all devoted their entire lives to studying, memorizing, and debating the Law, the Prophets, and the Psalms, that is, the Old Testament. Yet they missed it completely. They were constantly spitting Scripture at Jesus because He didn't seem to be following the rules very well.

Every time Jesus encountered them, He made it clear that they hadn't understood anything. Why? Because they were reading the Scriptures as if they were a rule book, not a revelation of God's love, wisdom, and character. They were reading the Bible with "correct doctrine" as their highest value rather than valuing real connection with the God who longs to know us and walk through life with us.

Let's summarize by comparing those two "trees" and what happens to us at each one.

At the Tree of Knowledge of Good and Evil . . .

- We're condemned and self-conscious. (Looking at ourselves and at others to see how we compare to them.)

- We're focused on what we know and don't know. ("Knowledge" is right there in the name of the tree.)

- We're focused on what we're doing right and wrong. (a.k.a. "good and evil," again, right there in the name.)

- Shame, guilt, striving, comparison, inferiority, fear, and insecurity are the fruit it produces in our lives.

- All of the above work together to rob us of confidence to approach God and enjoy Him.

- All of the above make us feel utterly disqualified from receiving God's promises.

The questions you tend to ask when reading the Bible at the Tree of Knowledge of Good and Evil are . . .

- What's the Rule/Principle I need to follow here?

- What's the "correct" process?

- What is my obligation to fulfill that will allow me to earn, merit, or deserve help from God?

At the Tree of Life . . .

- You become *God*-conscious instead of *self*-conscious.

- Your focus is on Jesus and what He's done for you and in you. (You become enthralled with who Jesus is. It's where He, "the Word made flesh," becomes the mirror through which you see who you really are.)

- You maintain a "righteousness consciousness" rather than a "sin, shame, and guilt consciousness."

- You stop framing your actions in terms of rule-following and law-keeping; but rather think in terms of being "responsive" to the promptings and instructions you receive from the Holy Spirit.

- What you see in the Scriptures feeds your confidence to run to God for help or simply for the sheer joy of being with Him.

- All of the above fills you with faith and confidence to receive God's promises. (You know you qualify because Jesus qualifies and you're "in Him.")

The questions you tend to ask when reading the Bible at the Tree of Life are . . .

- Father, what do You want to do today?

- Jesus, how do You want to reveal Your will and Your ways to me?

- Holy Spirit, where are You leading me?

Remember this...

The Bible is a wonderful, miraculous, life-giving gift from God. Which is why it is such a tragedy to try to read it in the light of the "wrong tree."

Lens #8

READ YOUR BIBLE

As Good News

Reframe it ...

The word gospel literally means "good news." The Bible is filled with it. Tragically, however, many people pick it up expecting shame, condemnation, or indictment. In other words, they expect bad news, not good. And we tend to "see" what we look for.

This chapter, this "lens," seeks to reveal the truth about the Bible. It's filled with good news. And the overarching, unifying theme is good news as well. The apostle Paul writes in Romans 10:15, *"How beautiful are the feet of those who preach the gospel of peace, who bring glad tidings of good things!"* (NKJV).

One of the greatest and most influential British preachers of the 19th century, Charles Spurgeon, once said the gospel can be explained in seven one-syllable words: "He laid down His life for us."

As we've seen in some of the previous lenses, everything in the Old Testament is simply a preparation and prelude and prerequisite to the arrival of Jesus. And when He arrived, He successfully did everything necessary to unbreak all that had been broken so very long ago.

That means reading the Bible as good news means reading it from the "correct side of the cross." Let's explore what that means.

The death, burial, resurrection, and ascension of Jesus is the hinge on which the entire story of the Bible swings. All four of the Gospels (Matthew, Mark, Luke, and John) contain the account. Of course they do! It's the event around which everything in the Bible that came before it points forward and everything in the Bible that came after it points back.

Everything from Genesis chapter 3, where we see the fall of mankind, up through the day before Jesus died, was one way.

Everything in the Bible that follows Jesus' resurrection was different. The cross changed everything.

Which is why it's vital to read the Old Testament and the portions of the Gospels prior to the cross with that in mind, just as you discovered in our examination of the differences between the old covenant and the new one.

Before the cross, God's people were exhorted to *try* to be righteous. Thus, the objective was strict obedience. After the cross, believers are exhorted to embrace the reality that they have been made righteous *because* of the blood of Jesus. Thus, the objective became faith in what Jesus had accomplished for them.

Before the cross, God was "out there." After the cross, God the Son came to dwell inside of believers. In the Old Testament the Holy Spirit would sometimes be "with" or "upon" a person. But after the cross it became possible to be "filled with the Spirit."

This represents one of the most miraculous, wondrous things about salvation. It's an astonishing thing to ponder the reality that God, in the form of the Holy Spirit, actually lives inside of you. Paul had this in mind when he wrote:

> *Have you forgotten that your body is now the sacred temple of the Spirit of Holiness, who lives in you? You don't belong to yourself any longer, for the gift of God, the Holy Spirit, lives inside your sanctuary.*
> (1 CORINTHIANS 6:19, TPT)

Paul had something similar in mind when he wrote: *"My old self has been crucified with Christ. It is no longer I who live, but Christ lives in me"* (Galatians 2:20, NLT).

As you can see, the cross changed everything. We are in Christ and Christ is in us. We are wrapped in Jesus' own righteousness. Transferred from the domain of darkness into the kingdom of His beloved Son. No wonder they call it "good news"! The cross changed everything, so understand on which side of the cross the passage you are reading sits.

Have you ever tried to read a book starting from the back? It's an approach that might seem absurd. Yet it's a fitting metaphor for how some approach the Bible without considering the pivotal role of the cross.

Reading Scripture without the cross as the focal point is like trying to understand the ending of a story without everything preceding it.

The cross of Jesus Christ is the crucial juncture in the biblical narrative. It's a moment that brings clarity and purpose to everything that precedes and follows it. Before the cross, we see a world in need of redemption, a series of covenants, and prophecies pointing toward a Savior. After the cross, we find the fulfillment of those promises. A new covenant underpinned by grace and a call to live in the reality of a fully restored relationship with God.

To read the Bible from the correct side of the cross is to place this central event at the heart of our understanding of Scripture. It means recognizing every verse, from Genesis to Revelation, is part of a larger story — a story that finds its resolution in the life, death, and resurrection of Jesus Christ. This perspective doesn't just change how we read the Bible. It transforms how we live our lives.

In the pages preceding the cross, Scripture unfolds in anticipation, casting shadows toward the coming Messiah. The Law, given to Moses on Mount Sinai, outlined a covenant of righteousness, setting forth a standard of living that was holy, just, and good.

Yet, this covenant also served as a mirror, reflecting humanity's incapacity to attain righteousness through their own efforts. The sacrifices, festivals, and rituals prescribed in the Old Testament were symbols of the need for atonement (that is, the payment of the debt created by sin). They pointed towards the necessity of a more profound, enduring redemption.

A notable example is the "Day of Atonement." Israelites who wanted to be in relationship with God and have their sins forgiven had to annually bring an unblemished, perfect lamb to be sacrificed.

This powerfully points to Jesus, our once-and-for-all sacrificial Lamb. Hebrews 9:22 says, *"And according to the law almost all things are purified with blood, and without shedding of blood there is no remission"* (NKJV).

Both the Passover lamb of Exodus and the sacrificial lamb of the "Day of Atonement" pointed to Jesus, the once-and-for-all-time sacrifice for our sins. (See Hebrews 10:1–18)

Referring to Jesus, Revelation 5:12 further makes clear this truth: *"Worthy is the Lamb who was slain, to receive power and wealth and wisdom and might and honor and glory and blessing!"* (ESV).

On this side of the cross, we can know our sins — past, present, and future — have been completely washed away!

The cross of Christ is the axis upon which the history of redemption turns. At the cross, Jesus accomplished what the law could never achieve: the complete, once-for-all atonement for sin. In His death, Jesus took upon Himself the full weight of humanity's sin and the rightful wrath of God against it.

> The cross represents the moment where justice and mercy meet.

Where God's holiness and love are both displayed. It's the pivotal event that changes the narrative from striving for righteousness to receiving it as a gift. As Colossians 1:13–14 declares:

> *He has rescued us completely from the tyrannical rule of darkness and has translated us into the kingdom realm of his beloved Son. For in the Son all our sins are canceled and we have the release of redemption through his very blood.*
> (TPT)

Reading your Bible on this side of the cross means reading knowing that being born again made you a brand-new person (2 Corinthians 5:17).

That new person is a righteous person – not because you suddenly exhibit perfect behavior but because you've received Jesus' own righteousness as a gift. By the way, the term *righteous* means being so completely right with God that you can approach Him, hang out with Him, and ask things of Him at any time.

And reading your Bible on this side of the cross means embracing your identity as a person made completely righteous with Jesus' own personal righteousness. As 2 Corinthians 5:21 says, *"For God made the only one who did not know sin [Jesus] to become sin for us, so that we might become the righteousness of God through our union with him"* (TPT).

This new identity isn't something achieved by our own efforts but believed and received by faith.

The letters (sometimes called *epistles*) of the New Testament are filled with exhortations and encouragements to receive and embrace the gift of Christ's righteousness. These are not burdensome commands but invitations to experience abundant life.

Reading the Bible from the correct side of the cross transforms not only our understanding of Scripture but our entire approach to life. It moves us from a mindset of struggling to earn God's favor to one of living in the joy and freedom of His grace. It shifts our focus from prideful self-righteousness to joyous, grateful acknowledgement of the gift of righteousness that is ours in Jesus.

So how can it be possible to read the Old Testament and early parts of the Gospels — which record events that happened before the cross — with a post-cross lens?

You do it by remembering what we learned in Lens #3, the section titled "Read Your Bible With an Understanding of the Two Covenants." There, we learned that all the promises in the old covenant were *conditional* promises. They were conditional upon a person's obedience to the Law.

Well, those of us standing on this side of the cross, if we're born again, have received the gift of Jesus' own righteousness. Put another way, Jesus fulfilled all the requirements of the Law on our behalf. Because we're "in Him," we qualify for all of those promises. As we saw in the earlier section, Jesus is our "Conditions Meeter." Here is an example of what that looks like.

Say you're reading Psalm 5. You come to verse 12 and find a wonderful promise:

> Lord, how wonderfully you bless the righteous. Your favor wraps around each one and covers them under your canopy of kindness and joy.
> (TPT)

That sounds amazing. After all, who doesn't want to be wonderfully blessed? And have God's favor wrapped around them? And live under a "canopy of kindness and joy?" But then you read the verse again, and your heart sinks. This is one of those *conditional* promises. It's only for the "righteous" person.

And if you're not reading that verse from the far side of the cross, you will immediately disqualify yourself. After all, you know how far short your behavior has been from any imaginable standard of "righteousness." So you sigh and move on to the next psalm.

But those reading this verse from the far side of the cross are thrilled to find it. When they see that this wonderful promise is reserved only for the "righteous," they think, *Great! I have received the gift of Jesus' own righteousness. Because I'm in Him, I qualify for this promise!*

Lens #8: Read Your Bible As Good News   77

How can we be so sure that all of the conditional promises like this one belong to those who are "in Christ?" Second Corinthians 1:20 explicitly says so. Take a look:

> *For all of God's promises find their "yes" of fulfillment in [Jesus]. And as his "yes" and our "amen" ascend to God, we bring him glory!*
> (TPT)

Every promise in the Bible is yours "in Jesus." From God's perspective, He has already said "Yes" to all of them. The only thing that remains is for us to add our faith-filled "Amen."

Again, it's no wonder they call these realities "good news."

All of this means you can come to your Bible, not filled with dread at being shamed or scolded, but rather filled with faith and expectancy.

You get far more out of your time in the Bible when you come expectantly.

It doesn't matter whether you "felt" anything or had an explosive revelation while reading.

When you're standing on the far side of the cross, your born-again spirit is communing and communicating with the Spirit of God as you read and ponder the Scriptures.

So, consider how you approach the Bible. Do you pick it up in fear, shame, condemnation, and apprehension? Or do you read its pages with hope, faith, and expectancy for what God can and will reveal to you — knowing all of its promises are "Yes"?

In Isaiah 55:11, God declares:

> *"So is my word that goes out from my mouth: It will not return to me empty, but will accomplish what I desire and achieve the purpose for which I sent it."*
>
> (NIV)

The assurance that God's Word accomplishes what He intends can inspire us to engage with the Bible not with passivity but as an active encounter with divine wisdom, instruction, guidance, reassurance, and love.

A powerful way to make your faith and expectation come alive is by engaging in the practice of personalizing, praying, and declaring the Scriptures. This involves reading a passage and using it as a framework for giving it voice.

For instance, read Psalm 23 and pray it over your life. Personalize the text and invite God to make it a reality in your circumstances. It could be prayed like this . . .

Lord, You are my shepherd.

Because of you, I lack no good thing.

You bring me to a place of rest, restoring my soul and leading me in a path of righteousness because it's simply who You are.

Though there may be moments when darkness surrounds me, I don't have to fear. You are with me. Your strength and confidence comfort me. Even in the face of my enemies or obstacles, you anoint me with the power of the Holy Spirit and bless me abundantly.

Surely, I will experience Your goodness and mercy every day of my life. And into eternity, I will dwell in the safety and security of Your house. Amen!

Remember this...

For the new covenant believer, the narrative of the Bible is not one of a distant deity looking to punish. It's of a loving Father seeking to reconcile His children to Himself. To reconnect in order to bless and help.

May you experience the joy, peace, and transformation that come from embracing the good news of the Bible.

Lens #9

READ YOUR BIBLE

As a Love Letter From God to You

Reframe it ...

For kids who grew up in church, *"God is love"* (1 John 4:8, NKJV) is probably the first verse they ever learned. And it's a great place to start. The most widely known and recognized Bible verse in the world is probably John 3:16, in which Jesus Himself speaks of God's love for humanity and of His desire to rescue them.

> *"For here is the way God loved the world — he gave his only, unique Son as a gift. So now everyone who believes in him will never perish but experience everlasting life. God did not send his Son into the world to judge and condemn the world, but to be its Savior and rescue it!"*
> (JOHN 3:16–17, TPT)

The theme of the Bible, if you have eyes to see it, is God's love for people. You see love for humanity as His motivation for every act and choice. In a very real sense, the Bible narrative is a love story of a Father moving heaven and earth to recover His connection with His wayward children.

What is true in general, is also true for you, personally. God loves *you*. And keeping God's immense, unfathomable, unconditional love for you in view puts you in the right posture to understand the Scriptures.

In the vast tapestry of human literature, there exists no greater declaration of love than the Bible. That may be a dramatic statement, but it's true nonetheless. The Bible speaks of a profound and enduring love, a relentless pursuit, and the ultimate sacrifice. All penned by the hand of a Father seeking relationship with His lost children.

To understand the Bible as a love letter, we must first grasp the essence of its Author. This love isn't a passive or conditional emotion but an active, all-encompassing, unyielding commitment to the well-being of His creation. Every word, every action attributed to God in the Bible springs from this deep well of love. And it makes the Scriptures become a living testament to His desire for intimacy with us.

> The act of creation itself — the formation of the cosmos, the Earth, and all living beings — was motivated by love.

God created humanity in His own image, endowing us with dignity, worth, and capacity for relationship. With Him and with each other. Through creation, God communicated, "You are loved, valued, and purposed." As we've already discovered, the Garden of Eden was a place of perfect communion, where God walked with Adam and Eve in the cool of the day. Where God's love for humanity was first expressed and experienced.

However, this love story encountered early heartache. The rebellion of Adam and Eve, driven by the temptation to find fulfillment apart from God, broke this perfect relationship.

> Yet, even as He pronounced judgment, God whispered the promise of reconciliation.

The entire Old Testament is the unfolding of this promise, through covenants made with Noah, Abraham, and Moses, and through the prophets who spoke of a coming Messiah. These were not mere instructions, but love letters. Each affirms God's unchanging commitment to restore this broken relationship.

Even in the Old Testament passages that seem harsh or cruel, the undercurrent of God's love can be perceived if you have this lens in place. As noted in Lenses 3 and 4, the Old Testament can be viewed as the chronicle of a bloody battle between God and his bitter enemy, Satan, over whether or not God would succeed in carrying out His plan of redemption. It was in love for all mankind that God firmly and consistently steered the Israelites away from idolatry and tried to insulate them from pagan influences.

The Gospels reveal the most profound chapter of this love story — God's love made flesh in the person of Jesus Christ. In Jesus, the Word became flesh, healing, serving, and ultimately sacrificing Himself for our redemption. Jesus' life, death, and resurrection are the climax of God's love letter, demonstrating love in the most selfless act imaginable.

God moved heaven and earth to recover His relationship with humanity, offering not just the promise of reconciliation but its very fulfillment.

John 3:16 captures the gospel in a single verse. Jesus' declaration that *"God so loved the world . . ."* (NIV) is good news.

Romans 5:8–11 further tells us, *"But God demonstrates His own love toward us, in that while we were still sinners, Christ died for us. Much more then, having now been justified by His blood, we shall be saved from wrath through Him. For if when we were enemies we were reconciled to God through the death of His Son, much more, having been reconciled, we shall be saved by His life. And not only that, but we also rejoice in God through our Lord Jesus Christ, through whom we have now received the reconciliation"* (NKJV).

This divine love letter does not end on the last page of your Bible. It continues into your daily life. It calls you to respond to God's love, to accept His grace, and to enter into the intimate relationship with Him that was His goal from the very beginning.

As John wrote of Him, *"We love because he first loved us"* (1 John 4:19, ESV).

Remember this...

As you read the Bible through this lens, allow its words to penetrate your heart. Let the stories, parables, letters, and poems found within its pages remind you of God's love, His promises, His faithfulness, and His relentless quest to rescue you and every other willing heart. Let them be a source of comfort, guidance, and inspiration as you navigate the complexities of life.

In the quiet moments of reading, listen for the whisper of God's voice, telling you, "You are loved. You are valued. You are mine." Let this divine love letter transform your understanding of God, yourself, and the world around you. And may you respond to this great love with a heart open to receiving and sharing with others the love that knows no bounds.

Lens #10

READ YOUR BIBLE

With
"The Helper" –
The Holy Spirit

Reframe it ...

In the Gospel of John, chapters 13, 14, 15, and 16 contain some of Jesus' final words of instruction to His disciples just hours before going to the cross. He spent a large portion of that precious time telling them about the coming of the Holy Spirit.

For example, in John chapter 14, Jesus tells them:

> "I will ask the Father, and He will give you another Helper, so that He may be with you forever; the Helper is the Spirit of truth, whom the world cannot receive, because it does not see Him or know Him; but you know Him because He remains with you and will be in you."
>
> (vv. 16–17, NASB)

It is so significant that Jesus chose to introduce the person of God the Holy Spirit as the "Helper." The Greek word Jesus used in this passage is *parakletos*, and some translations use the English word "Comforter" or "Advocate." All of those words are valid, but the literal meaning of *parakletos* describes someone who comes alongside you, takes you by the arm, and leads you where you need to go. Which makes the word "Helper" perhaps especially appropriate.

Later on in the conversation, Jesus gives His friends some additional information about the role of the Holy Spirit, but this time, instead of calling Him "the Helper," Jesus calls Him "the Spirit of Truth" or, as The Passion Translation says it, "the truth-giving Spirit":

> *"There is so much more I would like to say to you, but it's more than you can grasp at this moment. But when the truth-giving Spirit comes, he will unveil the reality of every truth within you . . . and he will reveal prophetically to you what is to come."*
> (JOHN 16:12–13, TPT)

Imagine you are visiting an ancient city with a complex network of winding streets and hidden alleyways. Navigating this maze alone could be overwhelming, causing you to miss out on significant sights. Now, picture having a knowledgeable, local guide by your side. Someone who knows every hidden path, every forgotten history, and every secret. This guide could help you see beyond the surface, making the city come alive with delightful surprises and enriching experiences you could never have discovered on your own.

That is what it can be like to read the Bible with the Holy Spirit as your guide. He becomes your divine interpreter and companion through Scripture. He illuminates paths you might otherwise miss and deepens your understanding of what God is saying. But remember, only if invited and welcomed.

> As we've seen, Jesus promised that "the Helper" would lead us into all truth (John 16:13).

This truth-revealing role is so wonderful and important.

As Jesus pointed out, religious leaders of His day like the Pharisees, Sadducees, and scribes had an encyclopedic knowledge of the Scriptures but completely missed their real and life-transforming messages. They memorized large portions of the Old Testament. They studied the words endlessly, carefully parsing them for meaning.

Yet without the Spirit's help, they utterly failed to grasp the true essence of what God wanted from them and for them, and missed what the prophets predicted was coming. Which is why the world's foremost experts on the Old Testament Scriptures didn't recognize the Person those Scriptures had been pointing to when He, the Messiah, was standing right in front of them.

We shouldn't be too hard on them though, because until the Day of Pentecost — the day Jesus fulfilled His promise to send "the Helper" (Acts 2) — the Holy Spirit simply wasn't available the way He is today. Even so, many Christians today make a similar mistake. They try to read and understand the Scriptures without help, the Holy Spirit. They try to navigate the ancient city without the Guide who knows it intimately, who knows where the treasure is buried.

To read the Bible with the Holy Spirit means first inviting Him into the process. This invitation acknowledges that while our human understanding is limited, the Spirit's wisdom is limitless.

> As you open your Bible, start with a simple prayer, asking the Holy Spirit to speak to you.

This practice sets the stage for a reading experience that isn't just informative, but transformational. The Holy Spirit can stir our hearts to respond to the Word with appropriate action, turning reading into a catalyst for change.

When we read the Bible with the Holy Spirit, the fruits of this practice are evident in several ways:

> **Increased Understanding:** The disciples on the road to Emmaus experienced their hearts burning within them as Jesus explained the Scriptures (Luke 24:32). We too can find new depths in familiar passages with the Spirit's guidance. You can live a thousand lifetimes, and the same passage, through the Holy Spirit, has the depth to give you fresh insight, new understanding, and lead you in new ways to better your life.

Personal Application: The Holy Spirit helps personalize the message of the Bible, showing us how ancient texts apply to current circumstances. In other words, He can and will show you not only what a passage means but perhaps more importantly, what it means to *you* . . . today.

A Heart for God's Word: The Spirit cultivates a love for Scripture that goes beyond duty to delight. The Holy Spirit's role is essential for you to enjoy reading the Bible.

Despite our best intentions, there are days when the Bible can seem closed to our understanding.

> In these moments, the Holy Spirit assists by softening our hearts, clarifying our thoughts, and even correcting misconceptions.

He helps us overcome spiritual dryness by guiding us to scriptures that rekindle our passion for God and His Word.

Reading the Bible with the Holy Spirit is a continuous conversation where the Spirit speaks through the words on the page into our life situations. This divine dialogue fosters a growing relationship with God.

Scripture is the language, and life becomes the context in which this language finds expression.

A minister once said, "If you have not read your Bible in some time, and you begin to feel guilty, the Holy Spirit is not making you feel guilty." The Holy Spirit is simply reminding you that you are hungry. Your spirit and God's Spirit are one and feelings of guilt do not produce anything other than regret. But recognizing you are simply hungry for what really gives you true life, is what God wants you to understand.

Remember this...

As you continue to explore the Bible with the "Helper," do so with a heart open to learning, changing, and responding. The Bible, with the Holy Spirit as our guide, is a source of wisdom, encouragement, and revelation for living a truly abundant life.

Invite the Holy Spirit into your reading and watch the words on the page — and the experience of your days — come alive like you never imagined!

Lens #11

READ YOUR BIBLE

Knowing it is Alive and at Work in You

Reframe it ...

After getting this far into this guide, you are surely now aware that the Bible is unlike any other book ever written. It's unique in so many ways. One of those ways is revealed in Hebrews 4:12:

> For **the word of God is alive** and active. Sharper than any double-edged sword, it penetrates even to dividing soul and spirit, joints and marrow; it judges the thoughts and attitudes of the heart.
> (NIV, EMPHASIS ADDED)

Now the Bible isn't the only way God speaks — He also speaks through His Holy Spirit using an inward voice, through circumstances, and through other people — but it is the primary way. And when God speaks in any other way, it will never contradict a *correctly interpreted* passage in the Scriptures.

This makes having a thorough knowledge of the Bible, read through proper lenses like the ones you've been discovering in the guide, so essential. It gives you a standard by which to measure and evaluate other messages.

Having the Bible hidden away in your mind and heart also helps you know when the Holy Spirit is speaking to you.

Yes, God speaks through His Holy Spirit at times by giving you thoughts and impressions in your spirit. It's often been called a "still small voice." God also speaks simply but powerfully through the presence or absence of His peace in your spirit when you're about to make a decision.

But what does Hebrews 4:12 mean when it says the Word of God is "alive" or "living"? We get a major clue over in a scripture we've looked at previously — 2 Timothy 3:16:

> *All Scripture is God-breathed and is useful for teaching, rebuking, correcting and training in righteousness.*
>
> (NIV)

Some translations say all Scripture is "inspired by God," but the Greek word here does literally mean "God-breathed." It means God supernaturally oversaw and guided the creation of those original manuscripts that make up our Bible. It also means that the Holy Spirit can and will use them to speak directly to *you* about things specific to *your* life.

What's more, it means, as Hebrews 4:12 explained, God's words carry power — power to reach down into the deepest parts of who we are as humans to illuminate and reveal and sort out what's just our soulish thinking and what are ideas from God.

Here are a few ways this happens:

Guidance in Decision-Making: Just as a lamp sheds light on a dark path, the Bible can guide your decisions and help you navigate complex situations. Psalm 119:105 says, *"Your word is a lamp to my feet and a light to my path"* (ESV).

Comfort in Trials: During times of distress, the Bible offers relevant words of comfort. Such as Psalm 91:1–2, *"He who dwells in the secret place of the Most High shall abide under the shadow of the Almighty. I will say of the* Lord*, 'He is my refuge and my fortress; my God, in Him I will trust'"* (NKJV).

Correction: The Bible acts as a mirror, reflecting our innermost thoughts and motives. Also, Hebrews 4:12's comparison of the Word to a double-edged sword illustrates how Scripture can point out when our thinking is wrong, or we're headed in the wrong direction. Jesus bore the punishment for our sin. So, our heavenly Father doesn't correct us with pain or trouble or sorrow.

He corrects us with His voice. As Proverbs 6:23 says, *"For the commandment is a lamp and the teaching a light, and the reproofs of discipline are the way of life"* (ESV).

Confidence: We can be sure that when God speaks, it will come to pass. Isaiah 55:10–11 says, *"As the snow and rain that fall from heaven do not return until they have accomplished their purpose, soaking the earth and causing it to sprout with new life, providing seed to sow and bread to eat. So also will be the word that I speak; it does not return to me unfulfilled. My word performs my purpose and fulfills the mission I sent it out to accomplish"* (TPT).

Affirmation of Identity: In moments of doubt or confusion about our worth, the Bible affirms our identity as children of God. Romans 8:16 assures, *"The Spirit himself testifies with our spirit that we are God's children"* (NIV).

Empowerment for Purpose: The Bible prepares and equips us for every good work, making it not just a book of ancient texts but a tool for discovering how to live out God's purpose for us. (See 2 Timothy 3:17)

Mind Renewal: The Bible transforms our thinking as we engage with it. Romans 12:2 emphasizes this renewal, which happens as we allow the Scriptures to reshape our values, views, perspectives, and attitudes.

Receiving Hope and Encouragement: Romans 15:4 says, *"Whatever was written beforehand is meant to instruct us in how to live. The Scriptures impart to us encouragement and inspiration so that we can live in hope and endure all things"* (TPT).

Hope for the Future: Lastly, the Bible is a source of hope, offering assurance for eternal life through Christ. Scriptures like Revelation 21:4 give us a glorious picture of what awaits: *"And God will wipe away every tear from their eyes; there shall be no more death, nor sorrow, nor crying. There shall be no more pain, for the former things have passed away"* (NKJV).

To fully experience the Bible as alive and active, consider these practices:

Meditative Reading: Spend time not just reading the Bible but also meditating on its passages. Let the words sink in and ask the Holy Spirit to illuminate their application to your life.

Scripture Memorization: By memorizing Scripture, you allow the living Word to dwell in you richly (Colossians 3:16), ready to come to mind in times of need.

Regular Study with Others: Engaging with the Bible in community allows you to see how the Word is working in others' lives. This can provide new insights and shared experiences of God's active presence.

Remember this...

The Bible is not a lifeless rulebook or a static collection of doctrines. It's a living, God-breathed force for transformation. Each time you engage with it, know that it's at work in you, molding your spirit, shaping your thoughts, and aligning your heart with God's. As you continue to read and reflect on Scripture, do so with the awareness that it is not just you who is active in the process — the Bible itself is through the power of the Holy Spirit!

Lens #12

READ THE BIBLE

With Fresh Eyes and an Open Heart

Reframe it ...

You're probably familiar with the late evangelist Billy Graham, who preached to millions all over the world throughout his life and passed away in 2018 at the age of 99. Reverend Graham's wife of nearly 64 years, Ruth Bell Graham, died 11 years before her husband, at the age of 87.

One of Billy and Ruth's grandsons tells a touching story of visiting his grandmother shortly before she passed away. She had been largely confined to bed and her eyesight was failing. It had been a while since he had seen her, and when he was ushered into her bedroom, he was surprised to see three of the four walls of the room lined with shelving, and those shelves filled with large, white three-ring binders.

When he asked her what all of that was about, she pointed to a white binder on her lap and said, "All of these are my Bible." She opened it up and revealed a page of text filled with inch-high letters.

Born in China to medical missionaries, Ruth had read the Bible every day for as long as she had known how to read. However, her failing eyesight had stopped her from being able to read even the largest print Bible available; she desperately missed her daily time in God's Word. So, her husband Billy instructed the ministry staff to print the text of the entire Bible out for her in huge letters — a task that required more than a hundred large three-ring binders.

She told her grandson that she was still learning new things and finding fresh encouragement, hope, and strength in the words of her beloved Bible.

Here is a truth that might surprise people who don't understand the power and majesty of the Scriptures: We can never exhaust the Bible's treasures. A long lifetime of consistent reading leaves us no closer than on the day we first opened it up.

There is a lesson in that for you. Don't assume you understand the meaning of a verse or passage just because you've read it many times and think you know what it means.

> Come to your Bible with fresh eyes.
> Question your assumptions.

Question your understanding of the meanings of words and phrases. Imagine that you don't know what you know. It is easy for a wonderful scripture or passage to lose its power simply through familiarity.

In practical terms, try a new translation, or perhaps a paraphrase like *The Message* or a hybrid like *The Passion Translation*.

Remember this...

You could live 100 lifetimes of 100 years and go to God's Word every day and still not have mined all of its gold. You would still not have grasped, comprehended, or understood all the revelation available in it.

Read your Bible, knowing there is no end to comprehending all He is and all He has done for you. But whatever you do, read it.

PART TWO

How to Read
& Enjoy

Psalms: pgs 109–112

Proverbs: pgs 113–118

Song of Songs: pgs 119–123

The New Testament: pgs 124–250

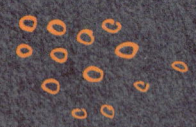

We've gathered the introductions for all 27 books of the New Testament as well as Psalms, Proverbs, and Song of Songs from The Passion Translation.

Before interpreting and applying, it is helpful to ask and learn: Who was the inspired writer of this book? Who was it written to? And what was the setting? What type of literature is this? What are the themes? Here you'll find the context to both prepare your heart and mind before you read, and to refer back to as you journey through the Scriptures.

HOW TO READ & ENJOY

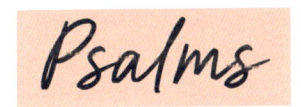

Psalms

AUTHOR:
Multiple authors, including David, Solomon, Asaph, the prophetic singers of Korah's clan, and Moses

AUDIENCE:
Originally Israel, but the Psalms speak to humanity in general

DATE:
From the monarchy to the postexilic era

TYPE OF LITERATURE:
Poems, which reflect several types: wisdom, lament, prayer, praise, blessings, liturgy, and prophetic oracles

MAJOR THEMES:
Praise, prayer, wisdom, prophecy, and Jesus Christ

OUTLINE:
The book of Psalms is really five books in one. Moses gave us the five books of the Law called the Pentateuch; David gave us the five books of the Psalms. Each division ends with a doxology that includes the word "Amen!" The last division ends with Psalm 150 as the doxology, forming an appropriate conclusion to this "Pentateuch of David." These five divisions have been compared to the first five books of the Bible:
- Psalms 1–41 (Genesis) — Psalms of man and creation
- Psalms 42–72 (Exodus) — Psalms of suffering and redemption
- Psalms 73–89 (Leviticus) — Psalms of worship and God's house
- Psalms 90–106 (Numbers) — Psalms of our pilgrimage on earth
- Psalms 107–150 (Deuteronomy) — Psalms of praise and the Word

ABOUT PSALMS

The Psalms find the words that express our deepest and strongest emotions, no matter what the circumstances. Every emotion of our hearts is reflected in the Psalms. Reading the Psalms will turn sighing into singing and trouble into triumph. The word *praise* is found 189 times in this book. There is simply nothing that touches hearts like the Psalms. Thousands of years ago our deepest feelings were put to music—this is what we all delightfully discover when reading the Psalms!

A contemporary name for the book of Psalms could be *Poetry on Fire*. These 150 poetic masterpieces give us an expression of faith and worship. They become a mirror to the heart of God's people in our quest to experience God's presence. Much of Christianity has become so intellectualized that our emotions and artistic creativity are often set aside as unimportant in the worship of God. The Psalms free us to become emotional, passionate, sincere worshipers. It is time to sing the Psalms!

PURPOSE

The Psalms are clearly poetic. They are praises placed inside of poetry. Everyone who reads the Psalms realizes how filled with emotion they are! You will never be bored in reading the poetry that spills out of a fiery, passionate heart. These verses contain both poetry and music that touch the heart deeply, enabling you to encounter the heart of God through your emotional and creative senses.

AUTHOR AND AUDIENCE

Most of these poetic masterpieces come to us from David, King of Israel. He wrote them during specific periods of his life: when he was on the run from Saul, grateful for the Lord's protection and provision, scared for his future, mournful over his sin, and praising God with uplifted hands. Other authors include David's son Solomon, Moses, Asaph, and the prophetic singers of Korah's clan.

While they were written during specific periods in the history of Israel—from the monarchy to the postexilic eras—they connect to our own time as much as they reflect their time. So in many ways these poems are written to you and me. The original audience was the children of Israel, but the Psalms reflect the hopes and dreams, fears and failures of humanity in general.

MAJOR THEMES

Poetry of Praise. The Psalms are pure praise, inspired by the breath of God. Praise is a matter of life and breath. As long as we have breath we are told to praise the Lord. The Psalms release a flood of God-inspired insights that will lift heaviness off the human heart. The Psalms are meant to do for you what they did for David: they will bring you from your cave of despair into the glad presence of the King who likes and enjoys you.

Poetry of Prayer. Mixed with intercession, the Psalms become the fuel for our devotional life. Each psalm is a prayer. The early church recited and sang the Psalms regularly. Many contemporary worship songs have been inspired by this book of prayer-poetry!

Poetry of Wisdom. The Psalms unlock mysteries and parables, for within the purest praise is the cryptic language of a wise messenger. The wisdom of God is contained in these 150 keys; you have a key chain with master keys to unlock God's storehouse of wisdom and revelation. It is the "harp" (anointed worship) that releases divine secrets. Read carefully Psalm 49:4: "I will break open mysteries with my music, and my song will release riddles solved."

Poetry of Prophecy. Prophetic insights rest upon the Psalms. David's harp brings revelation and understanding to the people. Singers who tap into the insights of the Psalms will bring forth truths in their songs, which will break the hearts of people and release divine understanding to the church. Prophets must become musicians and musicians must become prophets for the key of David to be given to the church.

Poetry of Jesus Christ. As with every part of the Old Testament, we are called to read the Psalms in two ways: (1) as the original audience heard them in their ancient Hebrew world; and (2) as the fulfillment of messianic prophesies, submitting by faith that these poems point to Jesus Christ. Therefore, at one level, these poems are all about him. There are 150 Psalms, and each of them reveals a special and unique aspect of the God-man, Christ Jesus. We could say every

Psalm is messianic in that each finds its fulfillment in Christ. Looking backward in light of Christ's revelation, we see they all point to our Lord Jesus, whom God has chosen as King over all.

Since these songs are all about Jesus, one of the keys to understanding the Psalms is to look for Jesus within its pages. Luke 24:44 says: "I told you that everything written about me would be fulfilled, including all the prophecies from the law of Moses through the Psalms and the writings of the prophets—that they would all find their fulfillment." There are many secrets about Jesus waiting to be discovered here!

HOW TO READ & ENJOY

Proverbs

AUTHOR:
Mostly Solomon, king of Israel, but other contributors too

AUDIENCE:
Originally Israel, but these words of wisdom are for everyone—they are written to you

DATE:
Pre-exile (chs. 10–29) and Post-exile (chs. 1–9; 30–31), the tenth to fifth centuries BC

TYPE OF LITERATURE:
Poetry and wisdom literature

MAJOR THEMES:
The fear of the Lord; God's transcendence and immanence; godly wisdom and human foolishness; the righteous and wicked wealth and poverty; men and women; husbands and wives; Jesus and wisdom

OUTLINE:
- Collection I. Introduction to Wisdom — 1:1–9:18
- Collection II: Sayings of Solomon, Part 1 — 10:1–22:16
- Collection III: Sayings of the Wise — 22:17–24:22
- Collection IV: More Sayings of the Wise — 24:23–34
- Collection V: Sayings of Solomon, Part 2 — 25:1–29:27
- Collection VI: Sayings of Agur and Lemuel — 30:1–31:31

ABOUT PROVERBS

The Bible is a book of poetry, not simply starched, stiff doctrines devoid of passion. The Bible, including Proverbs, is full of poetic beauty and subtle nuances ripe with meaning. The ancient wisdom of God fills its pages!

Proverbs is a book of wisdom from above tucked inside metaphors, symbols, and poetic imagery. God could properly be described as the divine poet and master artisan who crafted the cosmos to portray his glory and has given us his written Word to reveal his wisdom. Inspired from eternity, the sixty-six books of our Bible convey the full counsel and wisdom of God. Do you need wisdom? God has a verse for that!

Five books of divine poetry show us the reality of knowing God through experience, not just through history or doctrines. Job points us to the end of our self-life to discover the greatest revelation of the Lord, which is his tender love and wisdom. Psalms reveals the new life we enter into with God, expressed through praise and prayer. Next is Proverbs, where we enroll in the divine seminary of wisdom and revelation to learn the ways of God. Ecclesiastes teaches us to set our hearts not on the things of this life but on those values that endure eternally. And finally, in Song of Songs, the sweetest lyrics ever composed lead us into divine romance where we are immersed in Jesus' love for his bride.

The nature of Hebrew poetry is quite different from that of English poetry. There is a pleasure found in Hebrew poetry that transcends rhyme and meter. The Hebrew verses come in a poetic package, a form of meaning that imparts an understanding that is deeper than mere logic. True revelation unfolds an encounter—an experience of knowing God as he is revealed through the mysterious vocabulary of riddle, proverb, and parable.

For example, the Hebrew word for "proverb," *mashal*, has two meanings. The first is "parable, byword, metaphor, a pithy saying that expresses wisdom." But the second meaning is overlooked by many. The homonym mashal can also mean "to rule, to take dominion" or "to reign with power."

What you have before you now is a dynamic translation of the ancient book of Proverbs. These powerful words will bring you revelation from the throne room—the wisdom you need to guide your steps and direct your life. What you learn from these verses will change your life and launch you into your destiny.

PURPOSE

Within this divinely anointed compilation of proverbs there is a deep well of wisdom to reign in our lives and to succeed in our destiny. The wisdom that God has designed for us to receive will cause us to excel—to rise up as rulers-to-be on earth for his glory. The kingdom of God is brought into the earth as we implement the godly wisdom of Proverbs.

Although the book of Proverbs can be interpreted in its most literal and practical sense, the wisdom contained herein is not unlocked by a casual surface reading. The Spirit of revelation has breathed upon every verse to embed a deeper meaning of practical insight to guide our steps into the lives God meant for us to live.

AUTHOR AND AUDIENCE

You're about to read the greatest book of wisdom ever written, mostly penned by the wisest man to ever live. God gave Solomon this wisdom to pass along to us, God's servants, who continue the ministry of Jesus, the embodiment of wisdom, until he returns in full glory. While Solomon penned most of these words of wisdom, it is believed others had a hand too, including advisers to King Hezekiah and the unknown men Agur and Lemuel—which could be pseudonyms for Solomon. Regardless, the one who edited the final version of Proverbs brought together the wisest teachings from the wisest person to ever live to write a book containing some of the deepest revelation in the Bible. When Solomon pens a proverb, there is more than meets the eye!

To whom are these proverbs written? This compilation of wisdom's words is written to you! Throughout the book we find words like "Listen, my sons. Listen, my daughters." The book of Proverbs is written to us as sons and daughters of the living God. The teaching we receive is not from a distant god who tells us we'd better live right or else. These are personal words of love and tenderness from our wise Father, the Father of eternity, who speaks right into our hearts with healing, radiant words. Receive deeply the words of the kind Father of heaven as though he were speaking directly to you.

MAJOR THEMES

The wisdom found in Proverbs is about the art of successful living. The appeal of these insights is that they touch on universal problems and issues that affect human behavior in us all. Several major themes are present in these godly sayings of God's servant Solomon:

Lady Wisdom, Revelation-Knowledge, Living-Understanding. Throughout Proverbs wisdom is personified with the metaphor of Lady Wisdom, who dispenses revelation-knowledge and living-understanding. Lady Wisdom is a figure of speech for God, whose divine wisdom invites us to receive the best way to live, the excellent and noble way of life. Wisdom is personified as a guide (6:22), a beloved sister or bride (7:4), and a hostess who generously invites people to "come and dine at my table and drink of my wine" (9:1–6). In Proverbs, wisdom is inseparable from knowledge and understanding, which is not received independent of God's revelation. We are invited to "come to the one who has living-understanding" (9:10) in order to receive what Lady Wisdom has to offer. God promises that revelation-knowledge will flow to the one who hungers for the gift of understanding (14:6).

The Fear of the Lord. From the beginning, in 1:7, Proverbs makes it clear that we "gain the essence of wisdom" and "cross the threshold of true knowledge" only when we fear the Lord—or, as The Passion Translation reads, we live "in obedient devotion to God." Living in a way that our entire being worships and adores God is a constant theme throughout Proverbs.

God's Transcendence and Immanence. Proverbs teaches that God is both the author of (transcendent) and actor within (immanent) our human story. First, God is above and outside the world: as Creator "he broke open the hidden fountains of the deep, bringing secret springs to the surface" (3:20); "God sees everything you do and his eyes are wide open as he observes every single habit you have"

(5:21); he is sovereign and steers "a king's heart for his purposes" as easily as he directs "the course of a stream" (21:1).

Second, God is a part of and involved with the world: "The rich and the poor have one thing in common: the Lord God created each one" (22:2); "the Lord champions the widow's cause" (15:25); he "will rise to plead [the poor's] case" (22:23).

Proverbs teaches that God is all-powerful and transcendent while also taking part in our human story as our defender and protector.

Wise and Fool, Righteous and Wicked. Solomon believed there are basically two kinds of people in the world: the wise righteous and the wicked fools. The wise person possesses God's revelation-knowledge and living-understanding. Therefore, he is prudent, shrewd, insightful, and does what is right because he is righteous, a God-lover. This lover of God is just, peaceful, upright, blameless, good, trustworthy, and kind.

The wicked fool is different. He is greedy, violent, deceitful, cruel, and he speaks perversely. It's no wonder "the Lord detests the lifestyle of the wicked" (15:9)! As a foolish person, he is described as being gullible, an idiot, self-sufficient, a mocker, lazy, senseless, and one who rejects revelation-knowledge and living-understanding.

Many of Solomon's wise sayings relate to these two kinds of people, teaching us how to avoid being a wicked fool and instead live as God intends us to live, as his wise, righteous lovers.

Wealth and Poverty. As with many of Solomon's wise sayings, we cannot take one thought on wealth and poverty and apply it to every situation. Instead, Solomon teaches us seven major things about having wealth and being poor, and how wisdom and foolishness affect them both: the righteous are blessed with wealth by God himself; foolishness leads to poverty; fools who have wealth will soon lose it; poverty results from injustice and oppression; the wealthy are called to be generous with their wealth; gaining wisdom is far better than gaining wealth; and the value of wealth is limited.

Jesus and the Church. As with the rest of the Old Testament, we are called to read Proverbs in light of Jesus and his ministry. Throughout the gospels Jesus associates himself with wisdom. For instance, in Matt. 11:18–19 Jesus claims his actions represent Lady Wisdom herself. Where he is identified with Lady Wisdom in the New Testament, it is a powerful way of saying that Jesus is the full, entire embodiment of wisdom. In many ways Col. 1:15–17 mirrors Prov. 8. Likewise, the preface to John's Gospel resonates with this same chapter when Jesus is associated with the Word, another personification of wisdom.

Jesus stands at the center of Scripture; he can be found throughout Scripture, not just in the New Testament. So as you read these important words of wisdom, consider how they point to the One who perfectly embodied and is our Wisdom.

HOW TO READ & ENJOY
Song of Songs

AUTHOR:
King Solomon, king of Israel

AUDIENCE:
Every passionate lover of God

DATE:
The reign of King Solomon, 970–931 BC

TYPE OF LITERATURE:
Love poetry and wisdom literature

MAJOR THEMES:
Christ's divine love for his bride, divine Christian romance, and passionate Christian devotion

OUTLINE:
- Title of the Poem of Love — 1:1
- The Discovery of True Love — 1:2–16
- The Shulamite Finds Her True Identity as the Fiancée of the King — 2:1–7
- He Calls Her to a Higher Realm — 2:8–17
- She Endures the Dark Night of the Soul — 3:1–5
- The Revelation of the Marriage Carriage — 3:6–11
- How the King Sees His Bride-to-Be — 4:1–5
- The Shulamite Says Yes to the Higher Realm — 4:6
- The King's Perfect Partner — 4:7–5:1
- The Magnificent Bridegroom-King — 5:2–16
- The King Lives in Her Heart — 6:1–3
- She Ravishes His Heart — 6:4–10

Song of Songs 119

- The Radiant Bride — 6:11–7:13
- The Cup of Bliss — 8:1–4
- The Seal of Fire Placed upon Her Heart — 8:5–7
- The Vineyard of Love — 8:8–13
- The Divine Duet — 8:14

ABOUT SONG OF SONGS

We see the Shulamite's breathtaking journey unveiled in this amazing allegory. It is the path every passionate lover will take. But this divine parable penned by Solomon also describes the journey that every longing lover of Jesus will find as his or her very own.

To translate this portion of the Word of God, the Song of Songs, is to translate not only from a scholarly or linguistic perspective, but also from the passion of a heart on fire. Love will always find a language to express itself. Fiery love for Jesus pushes our thoughts out of hiding and puts them into words of adoration. This articulation, out of the deepest places of our hearts, moves God and inspires each of us to a greater devotion. Everyone deserves to hear and feel the passion of our Bridegroom for his radiant and soon-to-be-perfected bride.

The inspired Song of Songs is a work of art. It is a melody sung from the heart of Jesus Christ longing for his bride. It is full of symbols, subtle art forms, poetry, and nuances that the translator must convey in order to bring it forth adequately to the English reader.

Some of the cultural symbols that conveyed a rich texture of meaning to the Hebrew speaker nearly three thousand years ago have become almost impossible to leave in their literal form, since the English speaker of today has little or no connection to those symbols. This requires that much of the hidden meanings locked into the Hebrew text be made explicit. This is a dynamic equivalent translation—transferring the *meaning*, not just the *words*, into a form that many will find refreshing.

So be prepared to see yourself in this journey and hear the Lord's lyrics of love sung over you. Invest the time to read this through in one sitting. Then go back and read slowly and carefully, pondering each verse and praying through each love principle revealed in this translation. You may be shocked to read some of the things spoken over your life, considering them almost too good to be true.

PURPOSE

In reading this Shulamite's journey, the storyline's purpose is often missed or overlooked. The Holy Spirit has hidden within the Song of Songs an amazing story—a story of how Jesus makes his bride beautiful and holy by casting out her fear with perfect love. This sent-from-heaven revelation is waiting to be received with all its intensity and power to unlock the deepest places of our hearts.

Most of the earliest church fathers—including Origen, Gregory of Nyssa, Augustine, and Jerome—viewed the Song of Songs as a clear representation of Christ and his bride, presented in deeply symbolic and allegorical teaching. Along with many other early church fathers, they wrote commentaries to reveal the beautiful secrets given to us in Solomon's masterpiece.

Unfortunately for some, the Song of Songs has become merely a book expressing sexuality, with hidden meanings and symbols of sensuality. Many modern expositors teach from the Song of Songs the sexual relationship appropriate to a husband and wife. They find it difficult when others see the symbols and apply them to the spiritual journey every believer must take as we move further into the passionate heart of our heavenly Bridegroom. Their fear is that we "over-spiritualize" the Song of Songs. How hard that would be! How wonderfully spiritual and holy is this song of all songs!

AUTHOR AND AUDIENCE

The author of this love poem is made clear in the first stanza: "The most amazing song of all, by King Solomon." We can be thankful and grateful this wise, stately king gave us such a passionate, symbolic picture of the love of God—first for his people and then for Christ's church! Solomon's poetic insights deepen our understanding of the love of God in the same way they did for his people from generations past!

MAJOR THEMES

Interpreting Song of Songs. This divine song of romance is one of the most difficult books to interpret. Over the centuries there have been no fewer than six dominant ways people have understood Song of Songs, including typical, dramatic, mythological-cultic, dream, literal, and allegorical.

This translation reveals each symbol that the reader encounters in this song as a form of "virtual reality," an artistic masterpiece, which, when properly interpreted, helps us in our pursuit of Jesus Christ. Truly, if this is the song of all songs, its theme goes beyond and reaches higher than merely literal human sexuality. It extends to our union with the living God.

Christ's Divine Love for His Bride. The love of God shines and springs forth from the second verse in this poem of divine romance! It opens by testifying to the Spirit's kiss of God's divine word breathing upon us the revelation of this love, equipping us as his warriors and intoxicating us with his love.

This most amazing song speaks of God's saving love, keeping love, forgiving love, and embracing love. Even the allegory itself of the bride and Bridegroom-King speaks of the passionate pursuit of our loving God! Sitting with this poem of divine romance will transform your understanding of God's love like never before!

The dominant voice in this divine love poem is the Shulamite. The word *Shulamite* and the word for Solomon are taken from the same Hebrew root word—one masculine, the other feminine. We are one spirit with our King, united with him. He longs for his bride to be his love-prisoner, in the prison cell of his eternal love! Through our union with Christ we enjoy a joint possession of all things. You have become the Shulamite, and you will ultimately dwell in holy union with Jesus Christ.

Divine Christian Romance. This poem tells the story of our journey of divine romance as bride of the Bridegroom-King, Jesus Christ. It speaks of the journey every longing lover of Jesus will find as his or her very own. The bride sees her beloved as a shepherd, a representation of the relationship between you and your Beloved. The suffering love of Jesus will be in our hearts for the rest of our days—the revelation of our Beloved tied onto the cross like a bundle of myrrh, a picture of the suffering love of Christ dripping down from Calvary's tree for every lover of God.

The symbol of the bride (Christians) pursuing and being given to the Bridegroom-King (Jesus) also represents the *community* of brides, the church. For the beautiful bride overflowing with her Lover's life is to be given to others, even as Jesus was given to us by the Father. She has become a feast for the nations, wine to cheer the hearts of others. In this poem of divine romance the "city" is a picture of the local church, a place with government, order, and overseers. And the king's "vineyard" is a picture of the church, the multitude of those called to follow Jesus

Passionate Christian Devotion. Throughout this love song of divine romance, various symbols are used to speak of our passionate, emotional devotion to our Bridegroom-King-Lover: *lilies* are symbols of our pure devotion to Christ in the "temple" of our inner being; *foxes* are the compromises hidden deep in our hearts that keep the fruit of passionate devotion to Christ from growing within us; *hair* is a symbol of our devotion to Christ; *pomegranates* are equated to human passion and emotions, for when opened they speak powerfully of our hearts of passion opened to our Lover.

HOW TO READ & ENJOY

Matthew

AUTHOR:
Matthew, the former Jewish tax collector and disciple of Jesus

AUDIENCE:
Originally, the Jewish Christian church and the Jewish people

DATE:
AD 55–80

TYPE OF LITERATURE:
Ancient historical biography

MAJOR THEMES:
Gospel-telling, Old Testament fulfillment, heaven's kingdom realm, kingdom-realm living

OUTLINE:
- Jesus' Birth and Ministry Preparation — 1:1–4:11
- Jesus Teaches His Kingdom Realm — 4:12–7:29
- Jesus Demonstrates His Kingdom Realm — 8:1–11:1
- Jesus Is Opposed — 11:2–13:53
- Jesus Disciples His Disciples — 13:54–18:35
- Jesus Marches to the Cross — 19:1–25:46
- Jesus Dies, Rises, and Sends — 26:1–28:20

ABOUT MATTHEW

Four centuries of silence. Where was the promised Messiah? The Jewish people were waiting for the word of the prophets to come true, for they had prophesied that he would come. Then suddenly, the angel Gabriel made an appearance to a teenage girl to announce his birth. Shepherds saw a brilliant angelic light show on the hillside.

> Wise men went out in search of him.
> The light of the star shone over his manger.
> Insecure Herod wanted to kill him.
> Satan cruelly tested him.
> The prophet John presented him to Israel.
> God anointed him with the power of the Holy Spirit.

Then one day the King came into the synagogue and announced: "I'm here! I've come to set you free and to wash away sins, and liberate those who love and follow me."

We can thank God for Matthew, for in his Gospel he presents our eternal King. Matthew means "gift of Yahweh," and he lives up to his name. Thank you, Matthew, for the gift of your life and for what you have left for us in your Gospel!

PURPOSE

Matthew is a natural bridge between the Old Testament and the New because it has the most Jewish character. From the first verse to the last, Matthew establishes Jesus as a direct descendant of King David, preserving and fulfilling his royal line as the rightful heir as well as a descendant of Abraham, the father of Israel.

Furthermore, Matthew portrays Jesus as the new and greater Moses, who not only upholds the Jewish Torah but intensifies it—not in a legalistic way, but in a spiritual way, because following his teachings is the way into his heavenly kingdom realm.

It would be a mistake, however, to say there is only one purpose for this book. While one primary purpose is to communicate the Jesus story to the Jewish people, Matthew also means to communicate Jesus' story to us. One particular aspect of the Jesus story that Matthew wants to share is that Jesus is King of a heavenly kingdom realm. Mark and Luke also speak of God's kingdom realm, but Matthew focuses on how people behave as citizens of that realm, with Jesus as their loving King.

AUTHOR AND AUDIENCE

It is believed that Matthew may have been the first apostle to write a gospel, and he possibly wrote it in Hebrew (Aramaic). Though some maintain that Matthew wrote his Gospel after the destruction of the temple in AD 70, it's possible he wrote it anywhere from AD 55 to the mid-60s. He was a wealthy tax collector who profited greatly from his duty of representing Rome. And then one day, the man from Galilee stood in front of him and said, "Come, follow me."

There continues to be debate over the original language of Matthew's account. Eusebius, the Greek church historian, quoted Irenaeus as saying, "Matthew published his gospel among the Hebrews in their own language, while Peter and Paul in Rome were preaching and founding the church" (Eusebius, *Historia Ecclesiastica* III. 24.5–6 and V. 8, 2.) This, along with numerous other quotations from church fathers (Origen, Jerome, Augustine) would mean that the original manuscript of Matthew's Gospel was written in Hebrew. Regardless, it is without dispute that Matthew was a Jewish man who presents a Jewish King who now sits on the throne of glory for all people.

Perhaps an unbiased look at the Hebrew and Aramaic manuscripts would yield further nuances of our Jewish heritage as believers in *Yeshua* (Jesus) and would strengthen our understanding of the inspired Scriptures.

MAJOR THEMES

Gospel-Telling. The word *gospel* doesn't simply mean "good news." It is derived from the Greek verb *euangelizomai*, which means "to preach the good news." In other words, Matthew is writing to tell us heaven's truths embedded in the earthly events of the man Jesus. Matthew isn't giving us dry theology, but sharing stories and teachings designed in such a way as to unfold the majestic, magisterial person of Jesus, who embodies all of our theologies!

Old Testament. As the first book of the New Testament, Matthew connects the past with the present and with the future. He quotes sixty times from the Old

Testament, showing us that the New was enfolded in the Old, while the New Testament is the Old Testament unfolded and explained. The Old Testament is more central in Matthew than in any other Gospel, both in frequency and in emphasis. If the Jewish story is always pointing forward, Matthew's Gospel is its final act. It brings resolution to the Old Testament by presenting King Jesus and his kingdom realm and community as fulfilling their prophetic expectations.

Parables. There are unique components to Matthew's Gospel. For example, he records extensively the allegorical teachings of Jesus known as parables. Twelve are detailed by Matthew, and nine of them are unique to this account. He gives us two miracles of Jesus that are found nowhere else: the healing of two blind men and the miracle coin found in the fish's mouth. It is through these simple stories that the nature of both our King and his kingdom really come to life!

Heavenly Kingdom Realm. Matthew brings us the realm of the heavenly kingdom and sets its virtue and reality before us. The phrase "kingdom realm" is used nearly forty times as Jesus offers it to you and me. And Jesus is described as the King fourteen times. This is the Gospel of the King and his kingdom, but a different kingdom than even his followers expected. For the kingdom realm that Jesus ushered in would not liberate the Jewish people from oppression from the Roman government as they expected—we can define neither the King nor his kingdom ourselves. Instead, he offers not only Jews but every person access to an eternal, heavenly realm free from the consequences of sin and an oasis to refresh our lives!

Kingdom-Realm Living. Matthew's Gospel isn't only about our loving King and his kingdom, it's also about his subjects who act and live within that kingdom. The church is the community of Christ's heavenly kingdom realm, and Jesus' sermon on the hillside is the final Torah of the kingdom realm. For Matthew, a godly lover (the "righteous") is someone who has chosen to submit to Jesus as King and whose life is lived in accordance with his ethics. The Gospel of Matthew will bring before your eyes the power and majesty of our loving King. Encounter the wonder of Jesus as you read this book!

HOW TO READ & ENJOY

Mark

AUTHOR:
John Mark

AUDIENCE:
Roman Christians

DATE:
AD 50–55

TYPE OF LITERATURE:
Ancient historical biography

MAJOR THEMES:
The person of Jesus, the mission of Jesus, the work of Jesus, discipleship and faith, the kingdom realm

OUTLINE:
- Prologue — 1:1–13
- Jesus' Galilee Ministry: Phase 1 — 1:14–3:6
- Jesus' Galilee Ministry: Phase 2 — 3:7–6:13
- Jesus Leaves Galilee — 6:14–8:21
- Jesus Journeys to Jerusalem — 8:22–10:52
- Jesus' Jerusalem Ministry — 11:1–13:37
- Jesus' Passion — 14:1–15:47
- Jesus' Resurrection — 16:1–8 (9–20)

ABOUT MARK

God has given the world a treasure with the Gospel of Mark! What a beautiful description we find of Jesus, the Anointed One, within its pages. Mark unveils the

Lord Jesus before our eyes as the true Servant of God, holy, harmless, and merciful! As God's Servant we find Jesus very busy in this Gospel healing, teaching, and working wonders. You will fall in love with Jesus Christ as you read this inspired account of his life.

Many believe Mark was a disciple of Peter and received much of the material given in his Gospel from Peter, for Peter describes Mark as "my son" (1 Peter 5:13). The church fathers Papias and Clement of Alexandria both state that Mark wrote a factual and inspired Gospel with the help of Peter while Peter was still living. We know for sure that Mark wrote under the inspiration of the Holy Spirit and gave us a vibrant, striking picture of the life of the Messiah, Jesus, the Servant of the Lord. It is likely that Mark wrote this Gospel about AD 50–55. The book easily divides itself between Jesus' Galilean ministry (1:1–8:21) and his Judean ministry (8:22–16:8).

Mark omits the narrative of Jesus' birth and genealogy, for a servant needs no pedigree. But rather, he introduces Jesus as the one with a mission of love and power to change the world. Forty times Mark uses the Greek word *eutheos*, which means "immediately"! There is urgency with Jesus as he works toward completing his task of providing salvation and power to all who believe in him.

Mark records over three times as many miracles as parables. This is a Gospel of miracles! Twenty-one miracles are recorded here with two unique to Mark's Gospel. There is a freshness and vitality about this Gospel that is gripping to the reader. See if you can read the entire Gospel through in one sitting—you'll be on the edge of your seat! Although it is the briefest of the four Gospels, you'll still enjoy reading about Jesus' supreme power over both the invisible and visible worlds. He was with the wild beasts in the wilderness and subdued the even wilder nature of demon-controlled souls. He is Master over creation, man, and the devil, for he is the perfect servant who came to do the Father's will.

Mercy triumphs in every page of Mark's Gospel, for he writes as one set free from his past and as one who has discovered the divine surprise of mercy. May you also find mercy triumphant as you read the translation of this book. Today is the day for you to become a fervent follower of the Lord Jesus Christ!

PURPOSE

While John Mark likely had a variety of reasons for writing his Gospel, two broad themes stand out: (1) to confirm Jesus' messianic identity; and (2) to call believers to follow Jesus' example. The first purpose is confirmed by the dramatic moment (Mark 8:29) where Peter confesses, "You are the Messiah, the Son of the Living God!" The whole story pivots around this confirmation, though Jesus won't be confined to anyone's definition. Because while Peter and Israel expected a conquering hero Messiah, Jesus is the Suffering Servant Messiah. It is through the cross he achieves his full glory and full identity!

In his second purpose, Mark builds on his first by exhorting believers to follow Jesus' example. The disciples aren't the ones we are to model, however, for they repeatedly fail and remain relatively faithless throughout; their example is one to avoid! Instead, we are to pattern our lives after Jesus' own faithful, cross-shaped life. As Jesus said, "If you truly want to follow me, you should at once completely disown your own life. And you must be willing to share my cross and experience it as your own" (Mark 8:34).

AUTHOR AND AUDIENCE

The author of the Gospel of Mark is nearly universally recognized to be the John Mark who was related to Barnabas and lived in Jerusalem (Acts 12:12). He and Barnabas and Paul once traveled together in their missionary work (Acts 13:4) until some kind of failure took place in Mark's life and he left his team for a short period. Because of his abrupt departure, Paul refused to have Mark rejoin them from that time forward, which caused a rift between Paul and Barnabas. Even so, Barnabas the encourager still took Mark with him to advance the work of the gospel (Acts 15:36–39). It is also likely that Mark is the individual he mentions in Mark 14:51, using the common literary tool of that day when speaking of oneself by allusion.

Isn't it amazing how God does not give up on us because of our failures? It is comforting to see how God's mercy restored Mark and used him to write this inspired record, a gospel that will endure for all eternity. Later, while Paul was imprisoned, he asked Timothy to bring Mark to him, saying, "For he (Mark) is a tremendous help for me in my ministry" (2 Tim. 4:11). So we learn that none of our failures need disqualify us if we continue to love and follow Jesus Christ. When you get to heaven, ask Mark. He will tell you that mercy triumphs over judgment!

While the Gospels were written for the church at large, the writers often had specific audiences in mind and addressed needs and concerns relevant to them. Early Christian tradition closely identifies Mark's Gospel with Rome. This is supported by church fathers like Irenaeus and Clement of Alexandria. Since Mark translates Aramaic words into Greek for his readers and explains Jewish customs, a Palestinian audience seems to be ruled out. And because he uses Roman words in place of Greek ones, Christians in Rome were a likely target audience. He wrote to these Roman Christians to bring encouragement and assurance in their faith.

MAJOR THEMES

The Person of Jesus. Mark wrote his Gospel to write Jesus' story; the unfolding story itself reveals who Jesus is. He clues us into the revelation of his Person in the opening stanza: "This is the beginning of the wonderful news about Jesus the Messiah, the Son of God." These two titles, "Messiah" and "Son of God," point to what Jesus has come to do, which is key to understanding who Jesus is: He is the bearer of God's salvation, announced in words and deeds, teaching and miracles, and ultimately his sacrifice!

The Messianic Mission of Jesus. One of the most peculiar aspects of Mark's Gospel is the so-called "Messianic Secret." At various times Jesus commands his disciples not to reveal his true messianic identity. He tells others whom he's healed to keep his identity a secret too. In fact, the demons are commanded to keep the secret! Though he clearly demonstrated his identity through his miracle and teaching ministry, his full identity as Israel's awaited Messiah wouldn't be revealed until the end of Mark when he was resurrected in full glory.

The Work of Jesus. Some have said Mark is a Passion narrative with a lengthy introduction. Perhaps this is a bit of an overstatement, but Jesus' death plays a central role in this Gospel. While the work of Christ on the cross doesn't appear until the fourteenth chapter, Mark peppers references to Jesus' crucifixion throughout. He wrote to show that Jesus' death on the cross wasn't a tragedy or mistake, but God's plan from the beginning. Through suffering and death Jesus brings in the last days of God's kingdom realm. Through the crucifixion we see Jesus was both the long-awaited Messiah as well as the Son of God, which comes through the climactic confession of the Roman centurion: "There is no doubt this man was the Son of God!" (Mark 15:39).

Discipleship and Faith. At every turn in Mark's Gospel, Jesus is inviting people to follow him. This is the essence of discipleship. It's an invitation extended to everyone and anyone. Jesus taught that this kind of following involves three things: self-denial, cross bearing, and daily living. Denying oneself is about submitting to the lordship of Christ over every ounce of one's life. Taking up one's cross reminds us of Jesus' own self-denial on that cross of execution and his committal of himself fully to God's will; it is a radical and total commitment. Finally, following Jesus is a continuous, daily act that requires living out Jesus' teachings and example. This relationship is built on faith, which isn't some magical formula, but comes from a repeated hearing of Jesus' teachings and participation in his way of life.

The Kingdom Realm of God. "It is time for God's kingdom to be experienced in its fullness!" Jesus announced at the beginning of his ministry. "Turn your lives back to God and put your trust in the hope-filled gospel!" As with the other Gospels, God's kingdom realm takes center stage in Mark from the beginning where this opening stanza summarizes the good news Jesus brought. Later, in chapter four, Mark summarizes the entire ministry of Jesus and its effects with the term *kingdom*. The world is brought under "God's kingship" in and through the work of Jesus. For Mark the kingdom realm is already dynamically in the present, yet fully experienced in the future. It's surprising and small, yet powerful and great; beyond understanding for many, yet accessible to all; and calls people to a radical new way of living and challenges every human value.

HOW TO READ & ENJOY

Luke

AUTHOR:
Luke, beloved physician, friend, and companion to Paul

AUDIENCE:
Theophilus, and all "lovers of God"

DATE:
Late-AD 60s, though possibly 70–85

TYPE OF LITERATURE:
Ancient historical biography

MAJOR THEMES:
Jesus' person, Jesus' works, the kingdom realm, the Christian life, social dimensions, and the Holy Spirit

OUTLINE:
- Luke's Preface — 1:1–4
- Jesus' Birth and Childhood — 1:5–2:52
- Jesus' Ministry Preparation — 3:1–4:13
- Jesus' Galilean Ministry — 4:14–9:50
- Jesus Heads to Jerusalem — 9:51–19:44
- Jesus Teaches in Jerusalem — 19:45–21:38
- Jesus' Suffering and Death — 22:1–23:56
- Jesus' Resurrection and Exaltation — 24:1–24:53

ABOUT LUKE
You are about to read the biography of the wonderful man Jesus Christ. This glorious Gospel was penned by one of his early followers, a physician named Luke.

All four Gospels in our New Testament are inspired by God, but Luke's is unique. This could be described as the loveliest book ever written.

Luke's pen was anointed by the Holy Spirit and his book is still read today by the lovers of God, because it is the mercy Gospel. It is a book for everybody, for we all need mercy. Luke writes clearly of the humanity of Jesus—as the servant of all and the sacrifice for all. Every barrier is broken down in Luke's Gospel: between Jew and gentile, men and women, rich and poor. In Luke we see Jesus as the Savior of all who come to him.

Luke, being a physician, learned the need to exhibit compassion and mercy toward others. It comes through in every chapter. Luke's Gospel is perhaps the most compassionate and love-filled account of Jesus' life ever written.

Luke shares Jesus' teachings on prayer, forgiveness, and our obligation to demonstrate mercy and grace in dealings with others. Luke provides us with rich details of Jesus' love of children and the forsaken. Luke writes about Jesus' ministry to women twenty-four times. This was somewhat controversial in the culture of his day. In fact, Luke uses an alternating narrative of one story about a man and the next story about a woman. Luke begins with the story of Zechariah, then moves to Mary. A focus on Simeon, then on Anna. The Roman centurion, then the widow of Nain. The good Samaritan, then Mary and Martha. This pattern continues throughout his Gospel.

A large amount of Luke's Gospel is not found in any other Gospel narrative. If we did not have the book of Luke, we wouldn't know about the stories of the prodigal son, the good Samaritan, the wedding banquet, and other amazing teachings. Only in the book of Luke do we find the stories of the shepherds at Bethlehem, the ten lepers who were healed, the young man from Nain who was raised from the dead, and the dying thief on the cross next to Jesus.

Unveiled before your eyes will be the glorious man, Jesus Christ, and the revelation of his undying love for you.

PURPOSE

This world is a far better place because of the revelation Luke shares with us in his Gospel. He gives us a full picture of Jesus' life and ministry, applying scrupulous accuracy to all he wrote to ensure that what we read is factual. In fact, Luke uses the Greek word for "autopsy" (1:2) for investigating with firsthand knowledge those who had seen what Jesus did and heard what Jesus taught.

Dr. Luke performed an "autopsy" on the facts of Jesus' life, death, and resurrection, tracing them all back to their source to make sure what he compiled was of the highest degree of accuracy. He takes "Theophilus" through Jesus' entire ministry career to reveal how God worked to show Jesus to be true and the hope of the world. He also shows how God has been faithful to Israel and the promises he's given her, while inviting the nations to the table of Christ's love and hope.

AUTHOR AND AUDIENCE

We know little about Luke, the human author of this Gospel. He was a companion of the apostle Paul for some of his missionary journeys and was possibly one of Paul's early converts. Luke was a literary genius and writes with powerful prose. Some believe Luke was possibly the only non-Jewish writer of the New Testament. Others believe that he was a Syrian Jew who took upon himself a gentile name. It is obvious that he knew firsthand many of the early followers of Jesus, even the apostles who were chosen to preach his name throughout the nations. Near the end of the apostle Paul's life, when he was facing martyrdom, Paul wrote of his trusted friend, "only Luke [is] with me" (2 Tim. 4:11). Luke was mentored by the apostle Paul. This can be seen by Luke's vocabulary in his gospel. There are two hundred expressions or phrases that are similar in Paul's and Luke's writings.

The opening line of the Gospel indicates Luke wrote to the "most excellent Theophilus." The name Theophilus means "friend of God" or "lover of God." The Greek word means "most honorable" or "mightiest." Some scholars suggest there was no individual named Theophilus mentioned in Luke's writings. Regardless, Luke's Gospel is a greeting to all the lovers of God. He especially wrote it to non-Jewish lovers of God who may have felt out of place in the originally Jewish movement.

MAJOR THEMES

The Person and Work of Jesus. As you can imagine, a historical biography of Jesus will feature him and his work, front and center! In Luke's Gospel, he is the sent one who is both Lord and Messiah. He is uniquely and intimately connected to God, transcending any portrait of him as simply a human figure and agent. He is also the one who acts, as the promised Messiah anointed by the Spirit to bring in the new era—God's heavenly kingdom realm to earth. His ultimate act was on behalf of every person on the planet, bearing the sins of the world as he hung on the Roman cross. And in the end, this Lord Messiah was vindicated by the Father through the resurrection and exalted to his right hand through the ascension.

The Promised Kingdom Realm. In Jesus Christ, all of God's promises are fulfilled. Chief among them is God's promised kingdom realm. God's kingdom realm is both present and coming. Jesus commands his disciples to proclaim that it has "come near" and is within peoples' reach in the present. The promises of the last days have started to be fulfilled, and yet those promises haven't been ultimately fulfilled. The full manifestation of the kingdom realm is still anticipated, when all the hoped-for prophecies of restoration will be realized.

Women and the Poor. Women are a crucial part of Jesus' story—now and then. In Luke's Gospel they provide examples of deep piety and devotion. They are both of humble means and wealthy. At every turn women are part of Jesus' ministry: Elizabeth, Anna, and of course Mary play important roles in his infancy; women are healed, comforted, and forgiven in Galilee; on the way to Jerusalem, we meet Mary and Martha; and during Christ's most desperate hours, women weep at his feet, stand with him faithfully; finally, they receive the first revelation of Jesus' resurrection. Then there are the poor. Throughout Luke, the poor receive special attention too, showing that God deliberately reaches out to those whom society casts away. He makes clear the good news of Jesus and his love is for people like them, which means the gospel truly is for everybody!

The Holy Spirit. The Holy Spirit plays a major role in Luke's Gospel, where he is referenced nearly twenty times. The Spirit is the driving force in the picture Luke paints of God's coming salvation. He is the architect, the maestro guiding and energizing the events that transpire throughout the life of Jesus. We find him present from the very beginning with his conception and birth on to Christ's baptism in the Spirit and through to his powerful miracle ministry. One of the most important texts in all the Gospels is Luke 3:15–16, where John says one "mightier" than he would come baptizing with "the Spirit of holiness and . . . fire." This Spirit of fire is the sign and seal of the new era of the Messiah, come to rescue and re-create the world!

HOW TO READ & ENJOY

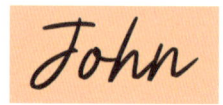

John

AUTHOR:
The apostle John

AUDIENCE:
Diaspora Jews and believers

DATE:
AD 80–85, though possibly 50–55
Type of Literature:
Ancient historical biography

MAJOR THEMES:
The person and work of Jesus, salvation, the Holy Spirit, and the end of the age

OUTLINE:
- Prologue — 1:1–18
- The Testimony of John the Baptist — 1:19–51
- The New Order in Jesus — 2:1–4:42
- Jesus as the Mediator of Life and Judgment — 4:43–5:47
- Jesus as the Bread of Life — 6:1–71
- Jesus as the Water and Light of Life — 7:1–8:59
- Jesus as the Light and Shepherd to Humanity — 9:1–10:42
- Jesus as the Resurrection and the Life — 11:1–54
- Jesus as the Triumphant King — 11:55–12:50
- Jesus' Ministry to His Disciples before Death — 13:1–17:26
- Jesus' Death and Resurrection — 18:1–20:31
- Epilogue — 21:1–25

ABOUT JOHN

How God longs for us to know him! We discover him as we read and study his living Word. But the "Word" is not just dead letters; it's the Living Expression of God, Jesus Christ. The Word came with skin on as the perfect Man—the One who is the divine self-expression and fullness of God's glory; he is God in the flesh!

The New Testament, at its beginning, presents four biographies to portray the four primary aspects of this all-glorious Christ. The Gospel of Matthew testifies that he is the King, the Christ of God according to the prophecies of the Old Testament, the One who brings the kingdom of the heavens to earth. The Gospel of Mark presents him as the Love-Slave of God, the perfect servant who labors faithfully for God. Mark's account is the most simple, for a servant doesn't need a detailed record. The Gospel of Luke presents a full picture of Christ as the true Man and the compassionate Savior of everyone who comes to him. And the Gospel of John unveils him as the Son of God, the very God himself, to be life to God's people.

We find miracles everywhere in the Gospel of John! Water became wine. Blind eyes were blessed with sight. Even the dead rose to walk again when Jesus lived among men. Every miracle was a sign to make us wonder about who this man truly is. The Gospel of John brings us a heavenly perspective filled with wonderful revelations in every verse. Nothing in the Bible compares to the writings of John. He was a prophet, a seer, a lover, an evangelist, an author, an apostle, and a son of thunder.

The other three gospels give us the history of Christ, but John writes to unveil the mystery of Christ. Jesus is seen as the sacrificial Lamb of God, the Good Shepherd, the Kind Forgiver, the Tender Healer, the Compassionate Intercessor, and the great I AM. Who can resist this man when he tugs on your heart to come to him? To read John's Gospel is to encounter Jesus. Make this your goal as you read.

There are three things that are important to remember about John, the author of this Gospel: First, John passionately followed Jesus Christ. He saw the miracles of Jesus firsthand and heard the anointed words he taught. He followed Jesus wholeheartedly, and became one of Christ's apostolic servants.

Secondly, John described himself as "the disciple whom Jesus loved" (John 21:7, 20). This does not mean that Jesus loved John more than the others; but rather, John saw himself as one that Jesus loved. You could also say about yourself, "I am the disciple whom Jesus loves!" Every single believer can echo John's description of himself, for these words must become the true definition of our identity.

Love unlocks mysteries. As we love Jesus, our hearts are unlocked to see more of his beauty and glory. When we stop defining ourselves by our failures, but rather as the one whom Jesus loves, then our hearts begin to open to the breathtaking discovery of the wonder of Jesus Christ. Jesus does not see us in the darkness of our pasts but in the light of our destinies!

And thirdly, it's important to keep in mind that John did not include everything that Jesus did and taught. In fact, if you put all the data of all four Gospels together and condensed it, we would have information covering merely a few months of Jesus' life and ministry! We are only given snapshots, portions of what Jesus taught, and accounts of a few of the miracles he performed. From his birth to the age of twelve, we know virtually nothing about his life; and from the age of twelve until he began his public ministry at thirty, we again have almost no information given to us about him in any of the Gospels. John summarizes his incomplete account in the last verse of his Gospel:

Jesus did countless things that I haven't included here. And if every one of his works were written down and described one by one, I suppose that the world itself wouldn't have enough room to contain the books that would have to be written! —John 21:25

John gives us the fourth Gospel, which corresponds to the fourth living creature mentioned in the book of Revelation—the flying eagle. This eagle brings before our hearts Christ as the One who came from heaven and reveals heaven's reality to those who love him. In Dan. 3:25, it was the fourth man walking in the fire who was in the form of the Son of God. This fourth man revealed in the fourth Gospel is the One who on the fourth day put the sun into the sky (Gen. 1:14–16).

According to Tertullian, one of the church fathers, John was plunged in burning oil in front of a massive crowd that had filled the Roman Coliseum in order to silence his ministry. But God was not yet finished with his aged apostle. Tertullian reported that John came out of the burning caldron alive and unharmed! This miracle resulted in the mass conversion to Christ of nearly all who witnessed it. John was later banished to the island of Patmos where he wrote the book of the Revelation of Jesus Christ.

You can trust every word you read from John, for he speaks the truth. His Gospel will take you into a higher glory where Jesus now sits exalted at the right hand of God. As John's Gospel unveils Jesus before your eyes, enter into the great magnificence of his presence and sit enthroned with him. Your life will never be the same after absorbing the glory presented to you in the book of John.

PURPOSE

The Gospel of John is all about the beautiful Christ. John tells us why he wrote this amazing book:

Jesus went on to do many more miraculous signs in the presence of his disciples, which are not even included in this book. But all that is recorded here is so that you will fully believe that Jesus is the Anointed One, the Son of God, and that through your faith in him you will experience eternal life by the power of his name! —John 20:30–31

John wrote with a twofold purpose: he's writing to nonbelievers, mostly Jews but also gentiles, to believe that Jesus is the One through whom they will find and experience eternal life; he's also writing to believers that they would more fully believe the same, to experience the fullness of that life by Jesus' powerful name.

The word *believe* is found nearly one hundred times in John. It is the Gospel of believing! We believe that Jesus Christ is the Living Expression of God and the Light of the World. He is the Savior, the King, the true Anointed One, the Living Bread, and the Loving Shepherd. This is why we continue to teach and preach from this magnificent, authoritative book: that people might have faith and grow in their faith. The Gospel of John reveals these living truths to us.

AUTHOR AND AUDIENCE

Many believe that John penned this Gospel about AD 80–85. However, the Dead Sea Scrolls hint at an earlier date as early as AD 50–55, since some of the verses found in the Dead Sea Scrolls are nearly identical to verses found in John's Gospel. The earlier date, though contested by some, seems to be more likely. Why would John wait to write and share the good news of Jesus? It seems likely that John wrote his Gospel prior to AD 66 when the Roman war with Jews began, for he mentions the Temple as still standing and the pool, which "has" (not "had") five porticos. The Roman army destroyed all of these during the Roman war of AD 67–70.

Jesus called John to follow him while John was mending a net, which seems to point to the focus of his ministry. John's message "mends" the hearts of men and brings healing to the body of Christ through the revelation he brings us.

There is an interesting possibility that both Jacob (James) and John (sons of Zebedee) were actually cousins of Jesus. By comparing Matt. 27:56 to Mark 15:40–41, we learn that Zebedee's wife was Salome. And Salome was believed to be the younger sister of Mary, the mother of our Lord Jesus, which would make her sons, Jacob and John, cousins of Jesus.

MAJOR THEMES

The Person of Jesus as God. Of all the major themes in John's gospel, the question of "Who is Jesus?" lies at its heart, especially when it comes to distinguishing it from the other three Gospels. For John, Jesus is the Son of God. He does only the things that God the Father tells and shows him to say and do (5:19). Jesus is God's unique Messenger, who claims to be God and yet submits to God. Through Jesus' obedience and dependence upon the Father, he becomes the center for disclosing the very words and deeds of God himself. Thus, the Gospel of John is as much about God as it is about Jesus!

The Work of Jesus in Salvation. John makes it clear that God the Father is the one who alone initiates human salvation. The one who bears the Father's salvation is the Son. Jesus is the Lamb of God, come to take away the sins of the world—which means we need him to save us from those sins. He is the Good Shepherd who lays down his life for his sheep. He is also the Bread of Life, the Light of the

World, the Way, the Truth, and the Life—all names that point to the salvation found in Jesus.

Faith features prominently in John's gospel, calling people to make a decision and confirm it by walking in the truth. More importantly, John teaches that such a decision merely reveals what God himself is doing in those who will eventually become his children—saving them through Jesus!

The Holy Spirit. The Spirit of God fills the pages of John in the way he fills the other gospels: the Spirit is given to Jesus at baptism, Jesus will baptize his people in this Spirit; Jesus is uniquely endowed with the Spirit; as the only one who has and gives the Spirit, Jesus shows us the characteristics of him. Above all, in this Gospel John connects the gift of the Holy Spirit to the people of God with the death and exaltation of the Son. We have come to know the precious doctrine of the Trinity in and through much of John!

The People of God. One of the major themes of John's gospel actually draws on the Old Testament: the formation of a people, a community that will embody and carry forth Jesus' mission. The community of God's people we call the disciples begins with a sort of commissioning, where Jesus breathes upon them, marking them as his new creation people. The act of breathing upon them recalls the original creation of the first human when God blew his breath into Adam. And like Moses' farewell address in Deuteronomy, Jesus addresses his followers (see chs. 13–17) to fulfill his redemptive purposes.

Believing in Jesus. The fact of the glorious life of Jesus Christ must lead us to faith in him. The word *faith* is found about forty times in Matthew, Mark, and Luke, but not once in John. Instead John uses "believe," a verb. He prefers to describe an action, not a state of mind or thinking. It is the Greek word *pisteuo*—believe! The claims of Christ on our lives require that we believe in who he is and what he has done. John speaks of this "believing" ninety-two times. For John, *pisteuo* means embracing Jesus and laying our lives on the words and deeds given to us by the Jewish Messiah. It means doing what he says.

Eternal Life Now and Later. As with the other gospels, John oriented his around the life, death, and resurrection of Jesus—the purpose of which is that humanity might have life—eternal life in the age to come, while experiencing a taste of it right now. Everlasting, unending life in this ultimate age is a gift God gives freely to people who believe in the redemption of Christ; the alternative is judgment. But this reality isn't merely for later, it's also for now; eternal life is both already and not yet. John emphasizes the present enjoyment of this eternal life and its blessings. But he also makes it plain Jesus will return to gather to himself his own to the dwelling he's prepared for them (14:2–3).

HOW TO READ & ENJOY

Acts

AUTHOR:
Luke, beloved physician, friend, and companion to Paul

AUDIENCE:
Theophilus, and all "lovers of God"

DATE:
Mid-to-late AD 60s, though possibly 70–85

TYPE OF LITERATURE:
Ancient historical biography

MAJOR THEMES:
Jesus, the Holy Spirit, salvation, the church, mission, persecution, discipleship, and social dimensions

OUTLINE:
- The Church is Born — 1:1–6:7
- The Church is Persecuted and Expands — 6:8–9:31
- The Church and Mission to the Gentiles — 9:32–12:25
- First Missionary Journey and Full Gentile Inclusion — 13:1–15:35
- Second and Third Missionary Journeys — 15:36–21:16
- Paul's Arrest and Journey to Rome — 21:17–28:31

ABOUT ACTS

The book of Acts provides us with the startling details of how the church of Jesus Christ began. We see the pillar of fire that led Israel through her wilderness years appearing in the upper room and splitting into 120 personal pillars of fire over the heads of the lovers of God. This inspired account of church history will awaken your soul with transforming power and give you courage to be a witness for Christ wherever he sends you!

Although many consider this book to be the "Acts of the Apostles," only two apostles are predominantly mentioned: Peter and Paul. It would be more accurate to call it the "Acts of the Holy Spirit." God indeed uses men and women to fulfill his purpose—those who are empowered, filled, anointed, and overflowing with the Holy Spirit.

Acts takes up the story where Luke leaves off. We begin with 120 disciples who had been in a ten-day prayer meeting. Acts explains the explosive beginning of the outpouring of the Holy Spirit that resulted in tongues, prophecy, miracles, salvations, and the birthing of countless churches. Acts provides us with the story of Paul's three missionary journeys, with many gentile nations hearing the gospel and believers being added to the church. Acts demonstrates the healing miracles of Peter, Paul, and the apostles. We see miracles in answer to prayers, including signs and wonders, and many deliverances. God will do what only God can do—and he is still working in power today through his yielded lovers.

We learn much about the Spirit of God in Acts. Without him, there would be no church, no evangelistic impact, no miracles, and no expression of the power of God. It is not by human means, human power, or human might, but by the limitless power of the Holy Spirit that God's kingdom realm advances on the earth; Jesus builds his church through the Holy Spirit.

PURPOSE

Like the book of Luke, Acts is a quick trip through history; it traverses the history of Christ's body, the church. Luke's purpose for writing was to offer a vivid portrait of the church's birth by cataloging the historical events in the movement of those who carried the good news about Jesus far and wide throughout the Mediterranean world.

The book of Acts confirms and further defines the identity of the church as the community of people who follow Jesus. Luke paints this picture with the Holy Spirit at the foreground, not background, of the church through the impartation of gifts and the miraculous signs and wonders that are present at every turn. He wants to make crystal clear that the life and work of Jesus continues on in the life and work of the church—which means it continues on in and through you and me!

AUTHOR AND AUDIENCE

Both Luke and Acts were written by a physician named Luke. The material in Luke and Acts covers a period of about sixty years, from the birth of Christ to the birth of the church and the early years of the expansion of God's kingdom realm on the earth. You could consider Acts to be "Luke, Volume 2," since he wrote them both for the lovers of God.

Luke wrote both of his books to someone named Theophilus, which means "lover of God." You are also meant to be the recipient of Luke and Acts, for Luke wrote them to you, the lover of God. You are the most excellent and favored one. He wrote his books for you!

MAJOR THEMES

Jesus, the Exalted, Exclusive Lord of Salvation. Acts opens in the same way Luke closes, with the ascension and exaltation of Jesus to the right hand of the Father. In essence, the disciples pick up where Jesus left off in seeing the salvation of the world realized. Not only is he the object of the church's affection, Jesus is the content of their message! Luke makes it clear that salvation is found in no one and nothing else but Jesus and his name. The word *name* appears over fifty times in Acts, signifying that Jesus is the exalted, exclusive Lord of salvation. We are saved through him and him alone!

The Holy Spirit of Power. There are almost four times as many references to the Holy Spirit in Acts as there are in the book of Luke. If Jesus was front and center in Luke, the Holy Spirit takes center stage in the book of Acts! He is the promised gift dispensed to Christ's disciples and unleashed through them on the world in full power. He enables the church to carry out its mission, empowers them to bear witness to the gospel, and anoints God's people to perform mighty wonders. The Spirit isn't reserved for the select, holy few; he is the promised gift given to all whom God has called and who believe in his Son.

Salvation for the World. The book of Acts makes it clear that "everyone who calls on the name of the Lord will be saved" (2:21). One of the most moving episodes is when Simon Peter is given a vivid dream from heaven. In this dream God essentially says the non-Jewish people Peter thought were unclean are now clean and also invited to partake of the same salvation he and the Jews enjoyed. Later the full council of church leaders realized the same thing: Salvation by grace through faith in Jesus was available to the entire world!

The Church, Mission, and Persecution. In a book about the birth of the church, one would expect to find more references to "church" than the twenty-three times this term appears in Acts. The reason is because Luke has a unique word for the church, a community called "the Way." His point is that the church of Jesus is a distinct community who are on a love-mission by the One who loves the world with fiery passion! For Luke, the church isn't merely a "gathering" or "assembly" (the English definitions of the Greek word); she's a movement—a Spirit-fueled movement led by leaders who articulate and apply the power of the gospel. And like most movements, the church faces opposition and persecution, yet triumphs and expands through the Holy Spirit's power.

Discipleship and Ethics in the Church. Discipleship is transformed in Acts because after Pentecost believers are able to follow Jesus in ways they couldn't before they received the Spirit. Because of the Spirit, this community is now an active community on an intentional mission to bear witness to the risen Christ in both word and deed. Proclamation is a central focus of this community in Acts. So too is their care for one another and the world around them in the name of Jesus. Such a commitment to the mission and message of Christ finds its expression in all their lifestyle. Through their love for neighbors and God, prayer, perseverance in suffering, watchfulness, faith, joy, and commitment to the lost, we find on-fire disciples of Jesus at every turn!

Women and the Poor. Luke continues the tone set in his Gospel here in Acts, insisting women are fully included in Jesus' work through his community of followers. They receive the Spirit of power in full measure, empowered as witnesses of who Christ is and what he did. In some contexts, women teach and prophesy. Luke makes it clear that unlike many social contexts, women are neither dismissed nor forgotten. Neither are the poor! While the term *poor* doesn't appear in Acts, we see the church rising up to provide for and care for them. Not only do they pool their resources together to care for the poor in their city, they send food along to other cities in need. They are gospel people who give out of the abundance of grace and mercy they've received from their heavenly Father!

HOW TO READ & ENJOY

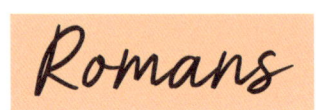

Romans

AUTHOR:
The apostle Paul

AUDIENCE:
The church of Rome

DATE:
AD 55–57

TYPE OF LITERATURE:
Ancient historical letter and theological essay

MAJOR THEMES:
The gospel, salvation, the love of God, justification, God's righteousness, the law, life in the flesh versus the Spirit, the destiny of Israel

OUTLINE:
- Letter Opening — 1:1–17
- The Human Condition — 1:18–3:20
- The Gospel Solution — 3:21–5:21
- The Gospel Freedom — 6:1–8:39
- The Gospel and Israel — 9:1–11:36
- The Gospel and Our New Life — 12:1–15:13
- Letter Closing — 15:14–16:27

ABOUT ROMANS

What you are about to read is a two thousand-year-old letter, penned by the apostle Paul and inspired by the Holy Spirit. You will be stirred, challenged, perhaps even corrected, as you read this enlightening letter. Paul's gospel was the gospel of grace and glory. When you receive the grace of God by faith, righteousness is birthed within your life.

The love of God is so rich; it leaves our hearts full of heaven. When we believe in Jesus Christ he pours his Holy Spirit into our hearts until every sense of abandonment leaves us. We become children of God, sons and daughters of glory, who follow the Lamb.

Do you want to be enriched and discover the heavenly treasures of faith, grace, true righteousness, and power? Plug into the book of Romans and you'll never feel the same again. Truth always sets the heart free, and nothing can free you more than the truth found in Romans. Grace and glory are waiting for you to unwrap and make your own. Live in the truths of Romans and watch how God's love sets you free!

The Protestant Reformation and the Wesleyan Revival both were born out of the revelation of righteousness found in Romans. Catch the fire of truth and grace as you read through Paul's masterpiece. While preaching in Corinth, Paul dictated the letter to Tertius (16:22) and entrusted it to Phoebe (16:1) to deliver it to the Roman believers. Phoebe was one of the outstanding women in the church of Cenchrea, a port city very near Corinth. We can date this letter to about AD 56. You can imagine the joy that came over the church at Rome when they read Paul's letter!

Read Romans a portion at a time, first overlooking the footnotes. Then go back and make a personal study with the hundreds of study notes we have included. You will be blessed as you read the anointed words found herein. The romance of Romans will fill you with freedom. Freedom from sin! Freedom from self! Freedom from dead works! A new freedom is coming into your spirit as you embrace the truth of Romans!

And you did not receive the "spirit of religious duty," leading you back into the fear of never being good enough. But you have received the "Spirit of full acceptance," enfolding you into the family of God. And you will never feel orphaned, for as he rises up within us, our spirits join him in saying the words of tender affection, "Beloved Father [Abba]!" For the Holy Spirit makes God's fatherhood

real to us as he whispers into our innermost being, "You are God's beloved child!"
—Romans 8:15–16

PURPOSE

Paul wrote Romans to communicate the grand themes of God's grace and glory encapsulated in the gospel! No one comes into glory except by the grace of God that fills believers with his righteousness. Our clumsy attempts to please God and our works of religion are totally unable to make us holy. But God is so kind, compassionate, and gracious that he shares his righteousness with all who receive his Son, Jesus Christ. He causes his faith-filled ones to be made holy by his grace and glory! Paul wrote his letter to clearly articulate this message, to explain why he preached it, and to show how it should impact Christians in their daily life and community.

AUTHOR AND AUDIENCE

Rome was the power center of the known world when Paul penned this letter. It was the most influential city on earth at that time. Although Paul had not yet been to Rome, he would one day be martyred there. So Paul wrote to these Roman Christians an important epistle filled with rich doctrines of our faith that reveal God's heart for his people, and what must be our proper response to such sacrificial love. Paul's theology flows from the romance of God toward us. Intimacy longs for understanding and oneness. And to be intimate with the God of glory requires that we understand his heart and join him in every way.

MAJOR THEMES

The Gospel. Arguably the central focus of Paul's teaching ministry is what Christians call "the gospel." It's also the major focus of his letter to the church of Rome. In the opening sentence Paul explains that God had set him apart with the mission to unveil "God's wonderful gospel" (1:1). This is one way of explaining the gospel. Here are some others: the revelation of God's Son; the wonderful message of Jesus; the joyful message of God's liberating power unleashed within us through Christ; the message of Christ's goodness, good news, and joyful news.

The Greek word for gospel is *euangelion*, which simply means "good news." Paul uses this word as shorthand for the amazing, joyful message of God's saving work in Jesus Christ. The entire Christian message is wrapped up in this one word. The gospel is the message about how God has acted in the world to rescue humanity from sin and death through the life, death, and resurrection of Jesus. So when Paul says gospel, he means all of that!

Salvation. God's wonderful salvation is presented to us in this letter—a salvation not of works or religious efforts, but the joyous salvation that comes to everyone who believes the good news of Jesus Christ. He has come to save us and set us free. This salvation is seen in Romans as comprehensive and complete, restoring our souls to wholeness and glory, through God's endless grace.

The Love of God. Paul sings of God's love throughout the book of Romans! He writes that right now we "experience the endless love of God cascading into our hearts through the Holy Spirit who lives in us!" (5:5). And this love is all because of Jesus: "Christ proved God's passionate love for us by dying in our place while we were still lost and ungodly!" (5:8). If you ever doubt God's love for you, plug into Romans to be overpowered by it, realizing we will never be deprived of this gift we have in Christ Jesus!

Justification. One of the most powerful words Paul uses to describe our new reality in Christ is the word *justified*. This is a legal term that basically means "to acquit." This is God's grace at its sweetest and most potent! While we were all at some point under God's wrath because of our sin, because Jesus paid the price of our sin in our place, we have been acquitted of all the charges against us and declared "not guilty" in heaven's courtroom!

The Righteousness of God. One of the most important themes of Paul in his letter to Roman Christians is righteousness, as it relates to both God and believers. He uses the word *righteousness* numerous times to refer to what we receive from God. Not only are we declared to be in the right, we are actually made right by God when we believe in Jesus. In fact, his righteousness is transferred to us through faith so that when we stand before God, that is who we really are: righteous!

The Law. Many have noted that Paul's relationship with the law is complicated (the Jewish law given by God to Moses for his people). In Romans, Paul says the law is "holy and its commandments are correct and for our good" (7:12). It was given to us for our benefit and intended to bring life, but instead it brought death (7:10). Paul concluded, "God achieved what the law was unable to accomplish, because the law was limited by the weakness of human nature" (8:3). Through Christ, God achieved what we could not: Christ perfectly fulfilled every requirement of the law so that now "we are free to live, not according to our flesh, but by the dynamic power of the Holy Spirit!" (8:4).

The Flesh versus the Spirit. One of the most interesting comparisons Paul makes is between our old life in "the flesh" versus our new life in the "life-giving Spirit." He offers this comparison as an exhortation to live the kind of life God desires from his children—not in the morally fallen way we once lived, but in the new way as true children of God "who are moved by the impulses of the Holy Spirit" (8:14).

The Destiny of Israel. From the very beginning Paul makes it clear that his joyful message of what Christ has done is for every single person on the planet: "the Jew first, and then people everywhere!" (1:16). Jews and non-Jews alike are under the same curse because of sin. Paul says the same solution to that problem is available for everyone by the same faith. While the Jewish people were given this promise first, people from every nation were later "grafted in" to share in their wonderful riches. And though Jews have fallen into unbelief, Paul makes it clear God will bring all of Israel to salvation once the full number of non-Jews have come into God's family!

PAUL'S LETTERS

Romans is the first in the canonical list of Paul's letters, which he wrote to churches to encourage, inspire, and instruct. No one demonstrated more care for the churches than Paul. Many of them existed because of Paul's ministry.

Each of the Pauline letters focuses on two major themes: the importance of right doctrine and the importance of right living. For example, Rom. 1–11 contain many instructions and teaching on having a proper belief system regarding sin, salvation, the work of the cross in our lives, God's endless love for us, and the place of Israel in the plan of God. It is only after Paul instructs the church that he encourages them to live holy lives. In other words, right understanding of truth is paramount in having a right understanding of how we are to live our lives for the glory of God.

Below is a list of the thirteen letters of Paul and the book of Hebrews (the author is anonymous, but traditionally the book is attributed to Paul). These letters, viewed as Scripture from the time they were written, account for over half of the New Testament that we have today.

- Romans
- 1 Corinthians
- 2 Corinthians
- Galatians
- Ephesians
- Philippians
- Colossians
- 1 Thessalonians
- 2 Thessalonians
- 1 Timothy
- 2 Timothy
- Titus
- Philemon
- Hebrews

Although each letter was written to a specific church or person or group, they were meant to be circular letters read by all the churches. Scholars believe they were all written within a span of less than fourteen years and are meant to bring all believers into the beautiful discovery of God's plan for their lives. They empower us today to live our lives with deep conviction of truth, faith, and love—overcoming every enemy and being victorious in Christ in all things. Amen!

HOW TO READ & ENJOY

1 Corinthians

AUTHOR:
The apostle Paul

AUDIENCE:
The church of Corinth

DATE:
AD 53–55

TYPE OF LITERATURE:
A letter

MAJOR THEMES:
The gospel, the church, spiritual gifts, holiness, love, and the resurrection

OUTLINE:
- Letter Opening — 1:1–9
- Causes and Cures of Division — 1:10–4:21
- Moral Issues and Marriage — 5:1–7:40
- Condemnation of Idolatry — 8:1–11:1
- Affirmation of Worship and Gifts — 11:2–14:40
- The Resurrection of the Dead — 15:1–58
- Letter Closing — 16:1–24

ABOUT 1 CORINTHIANS

The once influential seaport city of Corinth was strategically located at the crossroads of the world. Prosperous, powerful, and decadent, it was a city that God wanted to reach with the power of the gospel. God sent the apostle Paul to Corinth on his third missionary journey to establish a church in a city that desperately needed love and truth. Paul spent a year and a half in Corinth and saw the church grow, with more believers being added to their number daily. But they needed wisdom from their spiritual father, Paul. So he wrote this letter to encourage them to carry on in their faith and to remain steadfast to the truths of the gospel.

Written while Paul was in Ephesus, this letter had a powerful effect on the Corinthian believers. In his second letter to them, he was able to take them even further into the truths of our new covenant reality and the power of the gospel to overcome sufferings. While Paul was ministering in Corinth, he met two people who would become his coworkers: Aquila and Priscilla, a husband-and-wife team.

Perhaps this book is best remembered for the so-called love chapter. In 1 Corinthians 13 we have the clearest and most poetic masterpiece of love in the New Testament. God's unending love always sustains us and gives us hope. Think how many of the problems in your life could be solved by embracing the revelation of love found in this anointed letter of Paul! May the love of God win every battle in your heart, bringing a full restoration of your soul into the image of God, for God is love.

We are so enriched by having this inspired letter, written to Paul's spiritual sons and daughters. How grateful we are that God has given us the treasures found in 1 Corinthians!

PURPOSE

Many see 1 Corinthians as a letter of correction. Indeed, many errors had crept into the belief system of the church of Corinth and the spiritual walk of its members. Some of the issues Paul needed to address include: living godly in a corrupt culture, being unified as one body without competition, maintaining the priority of sexual and moral purity within the church, understanding more completely the role of spiritual gifts in the context of the church, embracing love as the greatest virtue that must live within our hearts, maintaining orderly worship with proper respect toward one another, and keeping the hope of the resurrection burning brightly in our hearts.

But 1 Corinthians is not all correction. Paul gave many wonderful teachings to the young church that will impact your life as well. Like the Corinthian believers, you possess every spiritual gift, you are fully equipped to minister to others, you are capable of demonstrating love to all, and the hope of a future resurrection brings meaning to your life today.

AUTHOR AND AUDIENCE

The apostle Paul wrote to the church of Corinth not as an outsider but as one who was intimately involved in their affairs as a founding father (see Acts 18). He composed this letter about AD 53–55, while living in Ephesus. He was responding to certain issues and problems in the Corinthian church. Apparently, a delegation had arrived from Corinth and notified Paul of what was taking place and asked for his advice. First Corinthians was his response.

While this letter was directed to a specific congregation in a specific Roman city, we are as much of the audience today, given how we mirror many of the characteristics that defined Corinth. It was considered a modern, cosmopolitan city; its people were staunch individualists; their behaviors reflected this individualism; their spirituality was polytheistic; and believers accommodated the gospel in ways that made it palatable to the surrounding culture. These characteristics could also be said of us.

Corinth was the New York, London, and Sydney of the ancient world. We need the voice of Paul and the Spirit of God to speak into our lives today. May we hear them clearly.

MAJOR THEMES

The Nature of the Gospel. This letter is gospel drenched! Not only in what it reveals about our story in Christ, but in what it reveals about his story too. In 8:6 we find revelation-truth about Christ that hadn't been understood before: "For us there is only one God—the Father. He is the source of all things, and our lives are lived for him. And there is one Lord, Jesus, the Anointed One, through whom we and all things exist." Here Paul equates the one true God of Israel, Yahweh, with Jesus. Jesus is Yahweh, the only true God.

Paul also revealed the nature of our story, the story each of us has committed to by believing the gospel. Paul shared the core message that had been part of the church from the beginning: "The Messiah died for our sins, . . . He was buried in a tomb and was raised from the dead after three days, as foretold in the Scriptures. Then he appeared to Peter the Rock and to the twelve apostles" (15:3–5). This is the essence of the gospel, the good news about our forgiveness from sins, freedom from shame and guilt, and new life in Christ. Like Paul, God's amazing grace has made us who we are.

The Church of Christ. One of the central issues Paul addressed was what we call ecclesiology, the nature of the church. What does it mean to be the people of God? What does it mean to gather as God's holy people—in Corinth, throughout America, or in Australia? One commentator declares these teachings on the church to be this letter's greatest theological contribution. As a church planter this makes sense. Paul was deeply concerned for his spiritual children and how they publicly professed and lived out the gospel in a gathered community.

In this anointed letter, Paul confronted the nature of church leadership and pastoral ministry. He addressed lawsuits that were tearing believers apart. He confronted head-on the toleration of sexual immorality within the community. And he addressed the nature of worship, particularly the expression of God's supernatural gifts that God has imparted to every believer. No stone is left unturned as Paul shapes our understanding of what it means to be "God's inner sanctuary" (3:16), literally "the body of Christ" (10:16) living and breathing in the world!

Holy and Ethical Living. In two of his other letters, Romans and Galatians, Paul made it clear that we are saved by grace through faith. In this letter, he makes it equally clear that we are "God's expensive purchase, paid for with tears of blood," and in response are called to "use your body to bring glory to God" (6:20). We do this by "following God's commandments" (7:19) and obeying "the law of Christ" (9:21).

No aspect of our new Christian ethics and holy living is left unaddressed. "People who continue to engage in sexual immorality, idolatry, adultery, sexual perversion, homosexuality, fraud, greed, drunkenness, verbal abuse, or extortion—these will not inherit God's kingdom realm" (6:9–10). We may be saved by grace, but Paul makes it clear that as Christians we are to live our lives in a way that glorifies and honors God (10:31).

Love, the Motivation of Our Lives. Each of Paul's letters seems to have an ethical high note. In his second letter to the Corinthians, it is generosity. In Ephesians, one could say it's humility. And Galatians emphasizes the fruit produced by the Spirit life. In this letter Paul uncovers the beautiful ethical prize after which we are to run: love. The so-called love chapter expounds upon the virtues of loving both God and neighbor, as Christ commanded. According to Paul, love is more worthy than speaking eloquently "in the heavenly tongues of angels" (13:1), better than having "unending supernatural knowledge" (13:2), and far more important than giving away everything to the poor (13:3). As Paul says, "Love never stops loving"; it never fails (13:8).

Issues of "the End." By "the end" we mean both our personal end at death and also our world's end when Christ returns. While we often think our end hope is in heaven, it isn't. Our ultimate Christian hope is in the resurrection. Paul spent fifty-eight verses and an entire chapter making this clear. In fact, this was his main message. Jesus' resurrection from the dead paved the way for our own resurrection. He is "the firstfruit of a great resurrection harvest of those who have died" (15:20). Because Jesus is alive, we have a bright hope for tomorrow. For this reason we can confidently declare, along with Paul, "Death is swallowed up by a triumphant victory! So death, tell me, where is your victory? Tell me death, where is your sting?" (15:54–55).

HOW TO READ & ENJOY

2 Corinthians

AUTHOR:
The apostle Paul

AUDIENCE:
The church of Corinth

DATE:
AD 56–57

TYPE OF LITERATURE:
A letter

MAJOR THEMES:
The person and work of Jesus, the gospel, the new covenant, Paul's apostolic ministry, Christian living, and generosity

OUTLINE:
- Letter Opening — 1:1–11
- Paul's Rift with the Corinthians — 1:12–2:13
- Paul's Apostolic Ministry — 2:14–7:16
- Paul's Collection Effort — 8:1–9:15
- Paul's Ministry Defense — 10:1–18
- Paul Speaks as a Fool — 11:1–12:10
- Paul's Final Warning — 12:11–13:14

ABOUT 2 CORINTHIANS

You are about to read a book written by a man who suffered for the cause of Christ, a man who knew trouble and how to overcome in victory. In 2 Corinthians you'll find a letter written by an apostle to a church that he planted—a church that needed a father's advice. In many ways, this letter serves as an apostolic manual for the body of Christ, replete with supernatural encounters, glory, love, and truth. This book is full of spiritual encouragement and revelation!

The church of Corinth had already received at least one prior letter from Paul. What we have in our New Testament as 1 Corinthians was Paul's second letter, making 2 Corinthians his third. The church had received Paul's rebuke in his prior letters, and now they were tender, open, and ready to receive all that their spiritual father had to impart. Although influenced by those who had claimed to be "super-apostles," their hearts were bound in love to Paul and the grace of God that was upon him.

How the church today needs the truth and love from this anointed apostle! As you read, picture yourself in the congregation in Corinth, hearing the letter read publicly. Let its truth penetrate your heart and stir you, as a new creation, to a greater passion to follow Jesus. Here you will find the wonderful secrets Paul learned about how to turn troubles into triumph. May you find more than you expected as you read through 2 Corinthians. Enjoy!

PURPOSE

Paul's letter to the church of Corinth is one of his most personal letters. In it, he wrote to defend his apostleship in the face of rival "super-apostles," as he called them, who were threatening the spiritual ground Paul had so carefully, paternally tilled. In defending his ministry Paul wrote to address a deeper issue with the Corinthian believers. He clarified how the gospel should impact every ounce of their lives, encouraging them to stay faithful to the truth and love that had been deposited in their hearts.

One truth the Corinthians had not yet grasped, which informed the purpose behind this letter, was their inability to fully embrace the scandal of the cross. The glory of the cross is the glory of the one who was crucified upon it. They had neglected to appreciate the self-suffering nature of the cross-centered life. So Paul passionately pointed to the glory that lies ahead, especially in the midst of weakness and suffering, stirring them to keep their eyes on the prize. What wonderful insights fill the pages of this letter, magnifying the majesty of Christ, which shatters the darkness, reconciles the lost, and recreates us anew!

AUTHOR AND AUDIENCE

Paul wrote this letter to a needy congregation in the Roman city of Corinth to bring them comfort, wisdom, and insight. Many believe that this letter is actually a compilation of two: a so-called "tearful" letter that makes up the ending (chs. 10–13), which was possibly sent before the main "reconciliation" letter (chs. 1–9). Apparently, a number of people had infiltrated the church of Corinth and challenged Paul's apostolic credentials and the gospel he preached, which had bearing on what they believed.

In this letter, we get a glimpse into Paul's own trials and the path of continual triumph that he discovered. He opens his heart to us in this book, sharing his deep emotions, perhaps more here than in any of his other writings. We learn of the magnitude of his sufferings as he informs us of the trials he experienced, which informed his understanding of the gospel. As a minister of reconciliation, Paul brings tremendous energy to the church through his letters. He is a true hero of the faith!

MAJOR THEMES

The Incarnation and Crucifixion of Christ. One of the major themes of this letter is the incarnate presence of Christ on earth. As Paul wrote, "Although he was infinitely rich, he impoverished himself for our sake" (8:9). Christ's coming and condescension to our lives reveals his "gentleness and self-forgetfulness" (10:1), but Christ is also clearly God (1:2). Christ's incarnation wasn't meaningless; there was a purpose to his impoverishment.

The Son of God came to earth "so that by his poverty, we could become rich beyond measure" (8:9). Jesus, who knew no sin, became sin for us, "so that we *who did not know righteousness* might become the righteousness of God through our union with him" (5:21). He was "crucified as a 'weakling,' " (13:4) yet he "now lives again" (5:15). Because he was, and because he does, "All that is related to the old order has vanished. Behold, everything is fresh and new" (5:17).

The Call of the Gospel. One of the clearest descriptions of the gospel's call on our lives is found in 5:18, "God has made all things new, and reconciled us to himself." Paul opens up the mystery of our being made right with God through the finished work of Christ on the cross. This call has gone out from God into the hearts of all his lovers: "Turn back to God and be reconciled to him." (5:20).

This gospel call is also heard in and through the ministry that God has entrusted to us, "the ministry of opening the door of reconciliation to God" (5:19). Amazingly, we are all "ambassadors of the Anointed One who carry the message of Christ to the world" (5:20). Through our words and deeds, it's "as though God were tenderly pleading with them directly through our lips" (5:20). Our motivation is to honor God and love Christ, while petitioning people on Christ's behalf to turn back to God and be made new.

Christian Ministry. This letter is one of Paul's most personal, because in it he exhibits the characteristics of a spiritual father who has been entrusted by God as a caretaker of his children. From the beginning he roots the compassion and comfort he passes along to others in God himself (1:3). His generosity as a laborer on behalf of the Corinthians flows from God's own generous hand (chs. 8–9). Paul is paternally devoted to his children, so much so that he feels their weaknesses and burns with zeal for their restoration (11:29). Like all parents, Paul's affection was clear: he was willing to "gladly spend all that I have and all that I am for you" (12:15). In many ways Paul outlines a theology of pastoral service that should be modeled and adopted by all ministers of the gospel.

The Christian Life. At the center of Paul's letter is a strong call to live a life of holiness; the Christian life is a holy life. He tells us not to "team up with unbelievers in mismatched alliances" (6:14). Which doesn't mean that we are to avoid befriending the world, but to avoid living like the world. We are to "come out from among them and be separate" (6:17). Holy living is deliberate living, for as Christians, we are called to "remove everything from our lives that contaminates body and spirit" and develop holiness within us (7:1).

Another aspect of the Christian life Paul addresses is the paradox of our Christian existence. We are comforted, yet afflicted; we are secure, yet we suffer; we are both strong and weak; we experience joy and sorrow; we die yet live. God "comes alongside us to comfort us in every suffering" (1:4). When we are at our weakest, we "sense more deeply the mighty power of Christ living in me" (12:9). And though "we continually share in the death of Jesus," his "resurrection life . . . will be revealed through our humanity" (4:10).

Christian Generosity. One aspect of Christian living that Paul highlighted is that of generosity. During his apostolic ministry, Paul spent a good amount of energy over the course of five years collecting resources for "the poor among the holy believers in Jerusalem" (Rom. 15:26). In this letter Paul made one more appeal to the church of Corinth. He attempted to stir them to greater love by issuing a challenge of generous giving. He compared Christian generosity to the "extravagant grace of our Lord Jesus Christ" (8:9). It is an "act of worship" (8:11) and maintains "a fair balance" (8:14) between believers. Christian generosity should "flow from your heart, not from a sense of religious duty" (9:7) and should be marked by enthusiasm and "joy," because "God loves hilarious generosity" (9:7).

HOW TO READ & ENJOY Galatians

AUTHOR:
The apostle Paul

AUDIENCE:
The church of Galatia

DATE:
AD 47–48, or early 50s

TYPE OF LITERATURE:
A letter

MAJOR THEMES:
Grace gospel, justification, the law, legalism, freedom and behavior, and Jesus Christ

OUTLINE:
- Letter Opening — 1:1–10
- Paul Defends His Ministry and Message — 1:11–2:21
- Paul Defends His Theology and Gospel   3:1–4:31
- Paul Applies His Message Practically — 5:1–6:10
- Letter Closing — 6:11–18

ABOUT GALATIANS

Heaven's freedom! This "grace gospel" brings heaven's freedom into our lives—freedom to live for God and serve one another, as well as freedom from religious bondage. We can thank God today that Paul's gospel is still being preached and heaven's freedom is available to every believer. We are free to soar even higher than keeping religious laws; we have a grace-righteousness that places us at the right hand of the throne of God, not as servants, but as sons and daughters of the Most High!

When Paul wrote his letter, the grace gospel was under attack. So too was his apostolic ministry—it was also debunked by those who wanted to mix grace with the keeping of Jewish law. Paul begins his letter to the Galatians by making it clear that it was not a group of men who commissioned him; instead, he was a "sent one" by the direct commissioning of our Lord Jesus Christ. And the message of grace that he preached was not a secondhand truth that he got from someone else, for he received it through a direct encounter with Jesus. Paul's ministry can be trusted and his gospel can be believed.

Who was this man, Paul? He was born with the name Saul in the city of Tarsus, the once prosperous capital of Cilicia in southern Turkey. Apparently there was a large Jewish colony in that region. Yet Saul was raised in Jerusalem and tutored by the venerated Jewish rabbi Gamaliel.

Before Saul was converted through a divine encounter, he was considered one of the most brilliant Jewish Pharisees of his day. After his conversion to Christ, however, his name became Paul and his ministry began. Reaching the non-Jewish nations with the glorious gospel of Christ was Paul's passion and pursuit. We can thank God that this brilliant man has left us his inspired letters to the churches.

PURPOSE

What a wonderful purpose is found in this letter from heaven! Shortly after the Holy Spirit was poured out upon Jewish believers in Yeshua (Jesus), the gospel spread to other ethnicities as well. By the apostolic mandate given to Jesus' disciples, they were sent into every nation. The first converts among the non-Jewish people needed clarity as to the "Jewishness" of the gospel. Was the gospel revelation to be based upon grace or upon keeping the law of Moses? Galatians was written by the apostle Paul to put those questions to rest.

AUTHOR AND AUDIENCE

The chronological order of the books of the New Testament is somewhat certain. However, the first book Paul wrote is often debated; some say it was 1 Thessalonians and others claim it was Galatians. It is my conclusion that Galatians was the first book he penned, possibly around AD 47–48, in order to passionately defend the gospel of grace from those who would confuse and twist the truth. The apostolic burden is always for purity, both in doctrine and in practice, which is why he confronted those who were distorting the gospel of Christ and reminded the Galatian church of the true message of grace.

MAJOR THEMES

Grace Gospel. When Paul wrote his letter proclaiming heaven's freedom, there were people perverting his original message of rescue from sin and death by grace through faith in Christ alone. These Judaizers, as they were called, added religious works to Paul's gospel, which placed non-Jewish believers under the thumb of religious bondage to Jewish laws. Thanks to Paul, we are reminded that a Christ-plus-something-gospel is no gospel at all; it is Christ-plus-nothing all the way!

Justification. One of the central issues for Paul in Galatians—and throughout his "Letters from Heaven"—is the issue of how people become right with God and find a "not guilty" verdict for their rebellion against him. The Reformation leader Martin Luther said that justification by grace through faith was the belief by which the church stands or falls. He's right! And Paul explains how it's possible a person can stand before a holy God without being condemned.

The Law and Legalism. The message of Galatians is clear: Christ's redemptive work on the cross prevents Jews and non-Jews alike from trying to become right with God through religious works; rescue and re-creation come on the basis of faith in Jesus alone. Through his grace, we are freed from the religious bondage that comes from laws and rituals.

Freedom and Behavior. The grace gospel brings heaven's freedom from religious bondage. Yet while Christians are free from the law, we are not free to live as we please. Instead, we are called to use that freedom to produce fruit, the "fruit of the Spirit," as Paul says. And it is through the Spirit of God that we not only find freedom but are also empowered to please God with our behavior.

Jesus Christ. As you might expect in a letter about salvation, Jesus Christ stands at the center of this letter. We see that Jesus is fully divine and should alone be worshiped. His cross also plays a pivotal role in Paul's grace-letter, for it is through his sacrifice alone that believers are made right with God.

HOW TO READ & ENJOY

Ephesians

AUTHOR:
The apostle Paul

AUDIENCE:
The church of Ephesus, and surrounding area churches

DATE:
AD 60–62

TYPE OF LITERATURE:
A letter

MAJOR THEMES:
Salvation and grace, God's power, church unity, and Christian conduct and identity

OUTLINE:
- Letter Opening — 1:1–2
- The Church's Heavenly Calling — 1:3–3:21
- The Church's Earthly Conduct — 4:1–6:20
- Letter Closing — 6:21–24

ABOUT EPHESIANS

What you are about to read is meant to be taught to every church. It is the constitution of our faith, the great summary description of all that is precious and esteemed in Christian doctrine and Christian living. Paul firmly plants the cornerstone of our faith in this powerful letter, cementing, in its few pages, the position and authority of the church over every other force. In it, Paul brings before every believer the mystery of the glory of Christ.

The theme of Ephesians is that God will one day submit everything under the leadership of Jesus Christ. He is the Head of the church and the fullness of God in human flesh. He gives his church extraordinary power to walk filled with the Holy Spirit, revealing the nature of God in all things. Jesus loves the church and cherishes everything about her. He is the one who brings Jews and non-Jews into one body. The church is God's new humanity—one new man. It is the new temple where God's glory dwells. And the church is the bride of Christ, the beloved partner who is destined to rule with him.

How wonderfully he blesses his bride with gifts from above. He gives us, both men and women, the grace to be apostles, prophets, evangelists, pastors, and teachers who will feed and encourage the church to rise higher. The greatness of God streams from Jesus Christ into the hearts of every believer. These are the grand themes of Ephesians.

PURPOSE

What an exciting letter Paul has written to us! Ephesians is full of life and its words reach higher in Christian thought than any letter in our New Testament. Full of living revelation, it simply drips with the anointing of the Holy Spirit. Where most of Paul's letters are addressed to churches facing specific issues dealing with belief and practice, this isn't the case with Ephesians. There is a more general, theologically reflective tone to this letter that is meant to ground, shape, and challenge believers (mainly gentile) in their faith.

AUTHOR AND AUDIENCE

Paul wrote this letter about AD 60, while in a prison cell in Rome, and sent it with Tychicus as a circular letter that was to be read to all the churches.

Originally, there were no titles on Paul's letters. They were gathered and the titles were assigned according to where they were sent; then they were published for the churches as a group. In none of the earliest Greek manuscripts did the words *Ephesus* or *Ephesians* occur. It was simply added in the margin next to the main text in the first copies made. The conclusion by some scholars is that this letter to the Ephesians may possibly be the lost letter of the Laodiceans mentioned in Col. 4:16: "Once you've read this letter publicly to the church, please send it on to the church of the Laodiceans, and make sure you read the letter that I wrote to them." Others believe it was intended for Ephesus as it stands today.

Scholars are not sure on this point; it is the only letter Paul wrote that did not contain any personal greetings to specific people. Since these greetings easily identified the other letters, many now believe this letter was written not only for the Ephesians but for Christians in the surrounding area too.

MAJOR THEMES

Salvation by Grace through Faith. Paul paints a very bleak picture of who we were before God stepped in to rescue us: "you were once like corpses, dead in your sins and offenses" (2:1). Yet he goes on: "Even when we were dead and doomed in our many sins, he united us into the very life of Christ and saved us by his wonderful grace!" (2:5). Paul makes it clear we don't earn or work for this rescue; rather, it's God's undeserved favor from beginning to end!

Power of God over All Others. One of the leading themes in this letter from heaven is the theme that God's power trumps that of all other principalities, powers, and authorities in this world. For Paul, any threat of the spiritual powers of this world should be seen in light of the superior power of God and the power we have as his children.

Christian Unity. Another leading theme in Paul's letter is the unity that Jews and non-Jews share in Christ. Paul's strong encouragement for unity and love within the body work together to encourage believers to overcome any and all cultural pressures of animosity on the basis of Jesus' work uniting all believers into one community of people.

Christian Conduct. Most of chs. 3–6 focus on how Christians should live, especially new believers, which is summed up with Paul's appeal in 4:17 to "not live like the unbelievers around you who walk in their empty delusions." Paul urges new believers—and really all believers—to cultivate a lifestyle consistent with their new life in Christ—a life free from drunkenness, sexual immorality, lying, stealing, bitterness, and other ungodly behaviors.

Christian Identity. One of the major themes of Paul's teachings is the fact that believers are now "in Christ," an idea that impacts every aspect of believers' identity. We exist in a personal, energizing relationship of unity with the risen Christ! This identity is crucial in our ongoing struggle with spiritual darkness and powers, maintaining Christian unity, overcoming our former lifestyle, and living as God has called us to live.

HOW TO READ & ENJOY

Philippians

AUTHOR:
The apostle Paul

AUDIENCE:
The church of Philippi

DATE:
AD 60–62

TYPE OF LITERATURE:
A letter

MAJOR THEMES:
The gospel of joy, Christ's lordship, Christian conduct, and Christ's community and identity

OUTLINE:
- Letter Opening — 1:1–11
- Paul's Gospel Priority — 1:12–26
- Gospel-Living Conduct — 1:27–2:18
- Examples of Gospel-Living — 2:19–30
- Paul's Gospel Experience — 3:1–21
- Final Encouragements — 4:1–9
- Letter Closing — 4:10–23

ABOUT PHILIPPIANS

What joy and glory came out of Paul's prison cell! Most of us would be thinking of ourselves and how we could get out; but Paul wanted to send to the Philippian church the revelation of joy!

The church of Philippi began because of a supernatural vision experienced by Paul while he was ministering at Troas (Acts 16:8–10). He had a vision in the night of a man from Macedonia who stood at his bedside pleading with him to come and give them the gospel.

It was in Philippi that Paul was arrested for preaching the gospel. Thrown in a prison cell and beaten, he and his coworker Silas began to sing songs of joy and praise to the Most High God! This caused a tremendous miracle as the prison doors were flung open and they escaped—but not before leading their jailor to Christ! Perhaps the jailor was the very man Paul had seen in his vision.

Philippi is where Paul met Lydia, a businesswoman who apparently led an import/export business from that city. The miracles of God birthed a church among the Philippians, and Paul longs to encourage them to never give up and to keep rejoicing in all things.

Paul's words point us to heaven. He teaches us that our true life is not only in this world, but it is in the heavenly calling, the heavenly realm, and in our heavenly life that was given to us through Christ, the heavenly Man. He left heaven to redeem us and reveal the heart of God, the heart of a servant. He gave us new birth that we would be heavenly lights in this dark world as witnesses of Christ's power to change our lives.

There is a good and glorious work that Christ has begun in our hearts and promises to complete once he is fully unveiled. Philippians teaches us how important it is to be joyful throughout our journey of becoming like Christ. The words *joy* and *rejoicing* occur eighteen times in this book. So read this heavenly letter of joy and be encouraged.

PURPOSE

This could be considered a letter written to friends. Throughout his Philippian letter, Paul speaks of unity and teaches how the church should live as one in the fellowship of Jesus Christ. We also discover in this, the warmest of Paul's letters, many truths about Jesus Christ, his humiliation and exaltation on high. Paul tells us that God seated us in the heavenly realm in his place of authority and power. No wonder we should have joy in our hearts!

AUTHOR AND AUDIENCE

Paul wrote this letter of heavenly joy about AD 60, while Timothy was visiting him in prison. Carried by one of the Philippian church leaders, Epaphroditus, it was delivered to the believers to be read publicly to all. He also wrote it to friends, to partners in the gospel, in the city of Philippi. Paul was motivated to write to these friends because of concerns he had over their disunity, suffering, and opponents. There were also two aspects of his imprisonment that cause him to write the letter: the gospel's advance while he was kept in chains, as well as the gift from the Philippian church. He wrote this letter to express his joyful faith in Christ Jesus while in prison and to communicate his appreciation and love for his generous friends in Philippi.

MAJOR THEMES

The Joyous Gospel of Christ. Paul's main theme in this letter is the gospel, a word that appears more often in this letter than any of his other letters. He is specifically concerned with believers' ongoing relationship with Christ on the other side of their acceptance of the gospel. He is also concerned with the advancement of the gospel, that Jesus' story of rescue and forgiveness goes out into all the world. The words "joy" and "gladness" are found nineteen times in this book!

The Lordship of Christ. At the heart of this letter is the famed *Christ Hymn* (2:6–11)—a soaring melody of worship, adoration, and revelation of the majesty and superiority of Christ as Lord over all. This hymn expresses in lofty, lyrical language the story of Jesus from his preexistent glory to the universal praise of him as Lord paved by his obedience to death on the cross.

The Conduct of Christ. Those who have received and believed the gospel are called to live according to the gospel, to conduct their lives in such a way that they live for Christ. For Paul, such a life is a process of seizing the surpassing worth of Christ and being seized by him. It is also a progressive pursuit of Christ in which we daily die with him in order to experience the fullness of his new life.

The Community of Christ. The community of Christ is the new people of God. Paul contrasts this new people with those in the old community who tried to bring non-Jewish Christians into the circle of Judaism. He also contrasts this community with the world, reminding believers that we are citizens of heaven who submit to the lordship of Christ. Finally, he reminds believers of their unity as brothers and sisters within God's household.

HOW TO READ & ENJOY
Colossians

AUTHOR:
The apostle Paul

AUDIENCE:
The church of Colossae

DATE:
AD 60–61

TYPE OF LITERATURE:
A letter

MAJOR THEMES:
Christ, the church, the gospel, and the Christian life

OUTLINE:
- Letter Opening — 1:1–2:5
- Letter Theme: Christ-Centered Living — 2:6–7
- Threats to Christ-Centered Living — 2:8–23
- Living a Christ-Centered Life — 3:1–4:6
- Letter Closing — 4:7–18

ABOUT COLOSSIANS

What a glorious hope lives within us! This is the theme of Paul's masterpiece written to the church of Colossae—our hope of glory!

The beauty and revelation that comes into us when we receive the truth of this letter is astounding. The Holy Spirit hands to us many wonderful nuggets of gold here. The heavenly hope of glory, the mystery hidden and reserved for this generation, is Jesus our anointed Messiah.

Paul penned this letter while in a prison cell. When hope was absent in his environment, Paul rediscovered it in his enjoyment of Christ within himself. No matter where you live or what surrounds you in this moment, there is a burning hope inside your soul that does more than just carry you through—it releases the heavenly Christ within. Great comfort and encouragement can be found by reading the letter to the Colossians.

Written about AD 60, Paul seeks to focus on the wonderful hope of the gospel and reminds the believers to not turn aside or fall victim to those who would minimize Christ and lead the church into empty philosophies and humanism. Already, there were many false teachers and cults that were forming and deceiving new believers and drawing them away from the supremacy of Christ. Many have noted that of all Paul's letters, Colossians speaks more of the importance of Christ than any other.

Nearly everyone who has studied Colossians would agree that the summary of this letter can be found in 1:18–19: "He is the Head of his body, which is the church. And since he is the beginning and the firstborn heir in resurrection, he is the most exalted One, holding first place in everything. For God is satisfied to have all his fullness dwelling in Christ."

We can never be moved away from our glorious Head, Jesus Christ! To see him is to see the fullness of the Father and the fullness of the Holy Spirit. How we love this firstborn heir of all things!

PURPOSE

The major reason why Paul wrote this letter was to equip the Colossian church to fend off false teaching and help them resist false teachers within the community. It seems as though certain Christians in the city had believed and were promoting a version of Christianity that threatened orthodox beliefs and practices that stood in contrast to what the Colossian church had received from Epaphras. Paul judged this version to not only be deficient but dangerous. He penned this letter to remind believers of the wonderful hope of the gospel and not to turn aside or fall victim to those who would minimize Christ and lead the church into empty philosophies and humanism.

AUTHOR AND AUDIENCE

Although the apostle Paul wrote this letter to the church of Colossae, we do not believe he was the one who started this church, nor had he ever been to the city. It was most likely the result of Paul's three-year ministry in Ephesus, which was less than a hundred miles away. So effective was Paul's preaching and teaching that his converts spread the message out of Ephesus throughout the region known as Asia Minor. Most likely it was Epaphras who was the church planter in the Lycus Valley, which included the cities of Laodicea, Hierapolis, and Colossae.

Although Paul had never visited their city, he had heard of the believers of Colossae and began to pray for them that they would advance and become the fullness of Christ on the earth. Perhaps the new converts had met first in the home of Philemon until they outgrew the "house church." How tenderly Paul speaks to them, as a father in the faith, to motivate them to keep their hearts and beliefs free from error. The church today needs to hear these truths.

MAJOR THEMES

The Supremacy and Centrality of Christ. The key theme to Paul's letter to the church at Colossae is the supremacy and centrality of Christ. One of the clearest pictures we have of this theme is the famed "Christ Hymn" of 1:15–20. Colossians makes it clear that in reigning supreme Jesus is himself God. As God he reigns over all creation. Paul also makes it clear that Jesus is all sufficient for our spiritual life, and should reign supreme at its center.

The Body of Christ. One of the most unique aspects of this letter is Paul's description of the church as Christ's "body." He presents Christ as the church's ruler, who has authority over her and who also sustains her. And as Christ's body, we are the continuing presence of Christ on the earth; through the church the mission of Christ is revealed and advanced.

The True Gospel. The major purpose for Paul's letter was to confront false teachers and their false gospel. Apparently, they were adding to the gospel Epaphras taught—mixing Jewish legalism, human tradition, and angel worship. Paul urges the Colossians to reject this religious enslavement and remember the true message of Christ and his lasting hope: "Never be shaken from the hope of the gospel you have believed in" (Col. 1:23).

The Christian Life. Using the metaphor of a body, Paul teaches that our life as Christians must be rooted in Christ—he is the Head, after all. He is the one who empowers us and renews us; we have our entire existence in him! Since it is through Christ we live as Christians, a "rules-oriented" lifestyle dictated by humans will not lead to spiritual growth.

HOW TO READ & ENJOY

1 Thessalonians

AUTHOR:
The apostle Paul

AUDIENCE:
The church of Thessalonica

DATE:
AD 50–51

TYPE OF LITERATURE:
A letter

MAJOR THEMES:
The gospel and faith, pleasing God, and the future

OUTLINE:
- Letter Opening — 1:1
- Thanksgiving for Faith — 1:2–10
- Ministry Explained, Thanksgiving Renewed — 2:1–3:13
- Exhortation to Christian Living — 4:1–5:11
- Letter Closing — 5:12–28

ABOUT 1 THESSALONIANS

What a fascinating letter! Full of encouragement and exhortation, 1 Thessalonians will leave you richer in your spiritual life. The apostle Paul brought the gospel to the important city of Thessalonica, with an estimated population of 100,000. Originally named Thermai ("hot springs"), the city was renamed Thessalonica, after Alexander the Great's half sister. The city was home to a Jewish community as well as many cults and false religions.

After leaving Philippi, during his second apostolic journey, Paul and his team arrived at the wealthy city of Thessalonica, the capital of Macedonia. As he preached and taught in the synagogue, many Jews and a large number of God-fearing non-Jews became believers and formed a congregation of Christ-followers. (See Acts 17:4.) But Paul and his companions had to cut short their stay, for their lives were in danger.

Shortly after leaving the city, Paul sent Timothy back to make sure the believers were doing well and living faithfully by the truths of the gospel. When Timothy returned, he informed Paul of the great faith, hope, and love that still burned in their hearts. So he wrote them this letter, about two years after the church had been established, in order to comfort and strengthen their hearts. The Thessalonians had let Paul know that they had questions about the appearing of Christ, so Paul addressed that subject in his letter. This was a young church that needed to hear from Paul.

Many scholars have concluded that 1 Thessalonians is one of the earliest known writings of the apostle Paul (along with the books of Galatians and 2 Thessalonians), which makes it perhaps the oldest Christian writing we have. It is dated back to AD 50–51, only twenty years or so after Jesus was crucified and raised from the dead.

In this deeply personal letter, Paul gives us wise and practical advice on how to live our lives with gratitude, grace, and glory. He speaks to the recipients as their "father" (2:11) and their "mother" (2:7). Eight times he addresses the Thessalonian believers as his beloved "brothers and sisters." He even describes them as his "exhilarating joy" (2:19).

Such a treasure is found in the few pages of this letter!

PURPOSE

Writing as a concerned "father" and longing "mother," Paul coauthored this letter with his fellow missionaries Silas and Timothy, to remind these dear believers in Thessalonica of what they had previously taught them and to reinforce what they already knew. After hastily departing them and finding no way to return, Paul dictated this letter to encourage them to maintain their hope in God by persevering, remaining pure, pursuing God's pleasure, and living in a way that prepared them for Christ's return. This concern is captured at the center of this letter:

Then your hearts will be strengthened in holiness so that you may be flawless and pure before the face of our God and Father at the appearing of our Lord Jesus with all his holy ones. (3:13)

Although Paul was encouraged by the Thessalonians' faith, hope, and love, he was still mindful of their vulnerability. So along with his trusted companions Silas and Timothy, Paul sent them this letter to build their spiritual muscles, help them live faithfully, and encourage them as they waited for Christ's return.

AUTHOR AND AUDIENCE

There is little doubt that Paul the apostle dictated the contents of the letter that was later sent to the Christian community at Thessalonica. In fact, many New Testament scholars consider it to be not only one of Paul's earliest letters but one of the earliest New Testament books. And yet Paul isn't the only author, for the letter opens with this: "From Paul, Silas, and Timothy. We send our greetings to you, the congregation of believers in Thessalonica." Paul and his coworkers jointly spoke into the situation faced by their audience, even though the letter was dictated by Paul.

Paul and Silas had a particularly special bond with the Thessalonians, for they had traveled to this Roman city from Philippi during their second missionary journey, after Paul received a vision of a man pleading with them to come. (See Acts 16:9–10.) During this evangelistic mission, a large number of God-fearing non-Jews, as well as many pagan idol-worshipers, turned to faith in Jesus Christ. Paul wrote these baby Christians and this infant church to encourage them to persevere, remain pure, and prepare for the coming of the Lord.

MAJOR THEMES

Faith and the Gospel, Explained and Personalized. While 1 Thessalonians isn't an apologia for the gospel, like Romans or Galatians, we still discover much about its essence. Paul speaks of it as a power (1:4) and as the Lord's message—a message not derived from the words of men but the very word of God (2:13), which was entrusted to the apostles (2:4). The gospel results in our being chosen and called by God (1:4; 4:7). The key verses of 1 Thessalonians are 1:9–10: "You turned to God from idols to serve the true and living God. And now you eagerly expect his Son from heaven—Jesus, the deliverer, whom he raised from the dead and who rescues us from the coming wrath."

Turning from idolatry and sin, toward God in faith and service, was their response to the gospel message that Paul, Silas, and Timothy preached—the good news that Jesus, our deliverer, rose from the dead, rescues us from God's wrath, and will one day return from heaven. This is reaffirmed near the end of the letter: "For God has not destined us to experience wrath but to possess salvation through our Lord Jesus, the Anointed One. He gave his life for us so that we may share in resurrection life in union with him" (5:9–10). There you have it: God's good news explained!

One of the more striking aspects of this letter is Paul's commendation of the believers' faith and the outworking of it in love and hope (1:3). He goes so far as to say that because of their faith, they had "become an example for all the believers to follow" (1:7). They had received the gospel "wholeheartedly," not as a "fabrication of men but as the word of God" (2:13), resulting in their lives being impacted by the gospel's power. Because of this faith, the Thessalonian believers were persecuted yet remained steadfast (3:7). You get the sense that Paul is inviting us to follow in their steps.

Living to Please God. The theme of living in a way that is worthy of the name "Christian" and in a way that pleases God runs strong through Paul's letters. First Thessalonians is no different. From the start, Paul commends these dear believers for putting their faith into practice (1:3). Yet he goes further, reminding them that as God's holy, set-apart people, they are called to live in a particular way.

First he challenges them "to adopt a lifestyle worthy of God" (2:12). When Paul first evangelized this community, this was part of what he taught them. So he reminds them of these teachings here and makes an appeal: "Keep faithfully growing through our teachings even more and more" (4:1). Why? Because "God's will is for you to be set apart for him in holiness" (4:3).

Finally, he reminds them that they are to live differently because they are different: "For you are all children of the light and children of the day. We don't belong to the night nor to darkness" (5:5). While living to please God can be difficult, especially in a culture that lives the exact opposite, it's something we're called to, something God desires from us.

Hopeful Preparation for the Day of the Lord. Paul wants us to be prepared in hope for the day when Christ returns in full glory. The main portion of Paul's letter is framed by this sense of waiting for, expecting, and being prepared for Christ's return. Paul praised the Thessalonians for eagerly expecting God's Son from heaven to rescue them (1:10). He exhorted them to be prepared for the day when he does return, keeping themselves completely flawless until his appearing.

In between waiting and keeping, Paul encourages the believers that those who have already passed away have not died in vain but died in hope—for God will bring with Christ those who have died in a declaration of victory!

He also wants them, and us, to "stay alert and clearheaded" (5:8) as we wait, for we don't know when it will happen. The Lord's return will come unexpectedly and as a complete surprise (5:2). Yet, though we may have questions about the end, we can be encouraged and encourage one another in the hope that we will "share in resurrection life in union with him" (5:10).

HOW TO READ & ENJOY 2 Thessalonians

AUTHOR:
The apostle Paul

AUDIENCE:
The church of Thessalonica

DATE:
AD 51

TYPE OF LITERATURE:
A letter

MAJOR THEMES:
Faith, perseverance, justice, Christ's return, laziness, and disunity

OUTLINE:
- Letter Opening — 1:1–2
- Thanksgiving and Prayer — 1:3–12
- The Day of the Lord — 2:1–17
- Idle and Disruptive Believers — 3:1–15
- Letter Closing — 3:16–18

ABOUT 2 THESSALONIANS

What will it be like to live in the last days before Jesus appears? What words of encouragement and warning would God want to give us? Paul's second letter to the Thessalonians gives us some answers. With only forty-seven verses, this book is packed with prophetic insight that will strengthen and prepare us for the coming days. Not only does 2 Thessalonians give us information about what is ahead, it is also a map to guide us through anything that might assail us as we approach the grand finale of all time—the appearing of our Lord Jesus Christ with his glorious messengers of fire!

Although we spend our lives watching and waiting for his appearing, we must live every day for his glory. We are to be alert, awake, and filled with his holiness as we draw closer to the fulfillment of the ages.

In this letter we find encouragement for us to stand our ground, be faithful to the end, and always make the message of Christ beautiful by our lives. We must do more than combat evil; we must live for Christ and expect his coming to find us as passionate lovers of God, abandoned to him with all our hearts.

Paul wrote this letter from Corinth around AD 51 (less than a year after writing 1 Thessalonians) to his beloved friends in the city of Thessalonica. They were followers of Jesus who looked to Paul as their apostolic father and were asking him to clarify the events surrounding "the day of the Lord." A faulty understanding of eschatology (the study of the last days) will lead to faulty conduct and even a detachment from our duties in this world. So Paul writes to inspire those who are idle to engage themselves with making a living and presenting the gospel of Christ through the holy example of their changed lives.

We all need the truth of 2 Thessalonians today to keep our lives focused on what is truth as we look to Christ alone to be our strength, no matter how difficult the future may appear. One day we will each be able to personally thank the apostle Paul for writing this inspired letter! May you be blessed as you read 2 Thessalonians.

PURPOSE

Building off of his first letter to the Thessalonian church, which he sent just a year or so prior, Paul gets down to business. It seems the situation had deteriorated in the short time between planting this Christian community along with his coworkers in the gospel and his first letter. So he wrote to encourage them in three main areas: to hold fast to their faith, despite opposition, knowing that God will act on their behalf with promised justice; to live faithfully as they awaited the coming of Jesus in glory; and to confront a group of "busybodies" (3:11) who were burdening and disrupting the life of the community.

Reading this letter, written to this threatened community, will remind us of the gospel's ultimate outcome—the glorious return of Jesus Christ—while helping us remain worthy of our calling by living our faith with conviction every day.

AUTHOR AND AUDIENCE

Although some have suggested 2 Thessalonians was written pseudonymously (written by someone other than Paul, who used Paul's name as his own), there are striking similarities between Paul's first letter and this one. Both contain an extended thanksgiving and a wish prayer, and both close with a prayer of peace. Although this letter lacks the warmth of 1 Thessalonians, it's clear the author already had a personal relationship with his readers. That makes sense if Paul was writing this as a follow-up letter to members of a community he founded, after a short period of time. Given how urgent the situation had become, Paul would have launched straight into his vital words of encouragement and exhortation.

This infant congregation of former pagans in the heart of the eastern region of the Roman Empire was struggling to understand their identity in Christ as well as how to live as God's people in a hostile culture. Knowing they faced a dire situation and confusion about vital issues related to the gospel and Christian discipleship, Paul addressed these dear believers with the care of a spiritual father.

MAJOR THEMES

Perseverance of Faith through Persecution. In his first letter to the Thessalonians, Paul acknowledged the suffering they were experiencing at the hand of a persecuting culture. He didn't want them to be unsettled by their trials, and he worried that might disrupt the gospel work he began among them and destroy their faith. Now he returns to this theme, praising them for their "unwavering faith" and boasting in their "unflinching endurance" (1:4) through all of the persecutions and painful trials they had experienced.

We aren't given specifics, but it seems persecution against these believers had ratcheted up significantly, so Paul wanted to encourage them that it wouldn't be in vain. Their perseverance of faith through persecution stands as a model for all the church, one we are urged to follow in endurance, to be counted "worthy of inheriting the kingdom of God" (1:5).

The Promise of God's Justice. In light of their persecution and trials, Paul wrote to encourage them that God hadn't forgotten about them. He would act on their behalf by judging their persecutors in the person of Jesus Christ (1:5–2:12).

Consider all that God has promised to do on our behalf to put things right: he will trouble our troublers, giving rest to those who are troubled. "He will bring perfect and full justice to those who don't know God and on those who refuse to embrace the gospel of our Lord Jesus" (1:8). The ungodly will suffer eternal destruction as a just penalty for their wicked ways, being banished from the Lord's presence. All believers will be adorned with glory. With this in mind, "live worthy of all that he has invited you to experience" (1:11).

Confusion about Christ's Coming Clarified. One reason Paul had written the believers in his first letter was to bring clarity as to what happens to believers at death and what will happen when Christ returns. Apparently, that letter didn't lessen their confusion! "Don't you remember that when I was with you I went over all these things?" Paul sarcastically writes. Apparently not! Therefore, Paul unveils further revelation-truth about what we should watch for and expect in these last days as we await the coming of our Lord in full glory.

As we wait, we're exhorted to "stand firm with a masterful grip of the teachings" we've been given, an "eternal comfort and a beautiful hope that cannot fail" (2:15–16).

The Lazy, Unruly, and Undisciplined. One might not expect believers who are lazy and disruptive, undisciplined and unruly, to be called out by Paul in such a short letter, yet they are. There's a reason: they "stray from all that we have taught you" (3:6), becoming a burden to the church. Such people refuse to work—"These people are not busy but busybodies" (3:11). The example of diligent, earnest work that Paul and his companions had set, and the teachings he laid out, were lifted up as a model for these believers. Since they themselves didn't sponge off the church, neither should anyone else. Since they worked hard to provide food and lodging for themselves, so should every believer. Paul's rule still stands: "Anyone who does not want to work for a living should go hungry" (3:10).

HOW TO READ & ENJOY

1 Timothy

AUTHOR:
The apostle Paul

AUDIENCE:
Timothy, Paul's spiritual son in the faith

DATE:
AD 62–63

TYPE OF LITERATURE:
A letter

MAJOR THEMES:
False teachers, false doctrine, church leadership, and God's household

OUTLINE:
- Letter Opening — 1:1–2
- Ordering and Organizing the Church, Part 1 — 1:3–3:16
- Ordering and Organizing the Church, Part 2 — 4:1–6:19
- Letter Closing — 6:20–21

ABOUT 1 TIMOTHY

First and 2 Timothy have been recognized as "Pastoral Epistles"—letters written by Paul for pastors and leaders to help them bring order and ordain elders (pastors) for the churches he planted. In fact, Timothy was an apostolic apprentice to Paul, mentored by a spiritual father who poured into his life, even after being sent out to establish churches and bring them to maturity. Timothy was the extension of Paul's apostolic ministry. Perhaps we should view these two letters more as "Apostolic Epistles" instead of Pastoral Epistles.

One reason we know that Timothy's ministry was unlike the pastoral ministry of today is that Timothy was an itinerant apostle who planted and brought healing and truth to the churches in which he ministered. Some of the locations he ministered in would include Thessalonica (1 Thess. 3:2–6), Corinth (1 Cor. 4:17; 16:10; 2 Cor. 1:19), Philippi (Phil. 2.19–23), Berea (Acts 17:14), and Ephesus (1 Tim. 1:2) His ministry eventually brought him imprisonment, much like his apostolic mentor, Paul (Heb. 13:23).

Timothy's name means "honored by God." He was from the city of Lystra, the place where Paul was stoned to death and then raised from the dead (see Acts 14:19–20). It may have been that Timothy witnessed what happened to Paul and was converted through what he saw. Paul recruited young Timothy and raised him up to take the message of the gospel to the nations. He soon began to travel with Paul in his missionary journeys and was eventually trusted with great responsibilities to teach and instruct the church.

Timothy was the son of a mixed marriage with a Greek father and a Jewish mother, whose name was Eunice ("joyous victory"). His mother was a convert to Christ and was distinguished by her faith. Timothy was likely in his thirties when Paul wrote him this challenging letter.

Timothy's ministry was in more than one location, for he was told to do the "work of an evangelist" in planting churches and winning souls to Christ. He was Paul's faithful representative to the churches of Thessalonica (1 Thess. 3:2), Corinth (1 Cor. 4:17), Philippi (Phil. 2:19), and Ephesus (1 Tim. 1:3)—yet it was in Ephesus where Paul left him to keep watering the seeds that had been planted to help the church there mature.

Paul instructs Timothy about the administration of the church and encourages him to hold up a high standard for those who lead. The qualifications for church leadership are spelled out in 1 Timothy (and Titus). And we are given clear instructions about caring for widows and for supporting the leaders of the church financially. Generally speaking, 1 Timothy could be seen as a manual for church planting. The key verse is found in 3:15: "But if I'm delayed in coming, you'll already have these instructions on how to conduct the affairs of the church of the living God, his very household, the supporting pillar and firm foundation of the truth."

What heavenly principles are revealed in this letter!

PURPOSE

The clear purpose of 1 Timothy is to reveal and emphasize the glorious truths of God. False teachers had begun to infiltrate the church of Ephesus, and Timothy was given the mission of preserving the truth and cleansing the church of error. Good relationships and spiritual growth can only come when the church grows in maturity and knows the difference between truth and error. There are wonderful revelations waiting for us in 1 Timothy that will focus our hearts on Christ, his glory, and his resurrection.

AUTHOR AND AUDIENCE

What beautiful words Paul shares with his spiritual son, Timothy! We are about to overhear the intimate words of encouragement and inspiration that a first-century apostle shared with his protégé. If we have any example at all of mentoring in the Bible, it is seen here in the relationship Paul had with Timothy. Written about AD 62–63, Paul imparts to Timothy the wisdom and revelation that is required to plant churches and lead an entire region into spiritual breakthrough.

MAJOR THEMES

False Teachers and Doctrine. Every generation has seen its fair share of false teaching; ours is no different, and neither was Timothy's. Paul commands him to confront false teachers and oppose unorthodox doctrines that "emphasize nothing more than the empty words of men" (1:6). He exhorts him to maintain his personal faith and warns against falling away, like others.

Qualifications for Church Leaders. In this letter to his ministry coworker, Paul has provided the church throughout the ages a helpful list of qualifications for two offices: overseers/elders and deacons. Both church officers are called to a similar standard of high moral and personal conduct, which includes integrity, peace, temperateness, generosity, and a well-managed household.

The Household of God. Throughout this letter from heaven, Paul explains what it means to live in the household of God. He outlines the proper treatment for widows, and he lays out the expectations for slaves, which can apply to workers too. He even says how the church should disciple its own. Paul gives Timothy the task of teaching Christ's vision for how his household should exist in the world.

HOW TO READ & ENJOY 2 Timothy

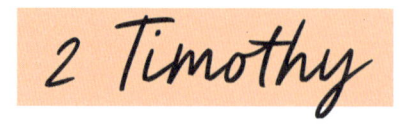

AUTHOR:
The apostle Paul

AUDIENCE:
Timothy, Paul's spiritual son in the faith

DATE:
AD 65–67

TYPE OF LITERATURE:
A letter

MAJOR THEMES:
False teachers, false doctrine, suffering, perseverance, and faithfulness

OUTLINE:
- Letter Opening — 1:1–2
- Thanksgiving for Timothy's Faith — 1:3–5
- Encouragement to Timothy — 1:6–2:13
- Instructions for Timothy — 2:14–4:8
- Letter Closing — 4:9–22

ABOUT 2 TIMOTHY

This could be called the last will and testament of Paul the apostle. Filled with warnings of the troubles that were ahead, this letter speaks to our generation with an unusual urgency. The outward display of religion must not entice the passionate and hungry, turning them away from the truth of the gospel. Paul's heart burns as he looks to the end of his journey and knows that death is near. He stirs our conscience with his emotional letter.

The urgency of this letter is Paul's revelation of the last days. Mentioned here in 2 Timothy more than any other letter, Paul warns, instructs, and challenges all of us to live a life of purity as the days grow evil. He gives us six analogies of the last days' servant of the Lord. The believer is compared to a soldier (2:3), an athlete (2:5), a farmer (2:6), a minister (2:15), a container (2:21), and a servant (2:24).

There are many verses that could be considered the most important themes of the book, but perhaps 4.7–8 would contain the summary theme of the letter:

I have fought an excellent fight. I have finished my full course and I've kept my heart full of faith. There's a crown of righteousness waiting in heaven for me, and I know that my Lord will reward me on his day of righteous judgment. And this crown is not only waiting for me, but for all who love and long for his unveiling.

As you read 2 Timothy, try to picture Paul sitting in a prison cell. He misses his wonderful disciple Timothy. Picture Timothy reading this letter with a longing deep within to hear these final words from his spiritual dad. Their love is deep, their commitment to the gospel is powerful, and their desire to see the world reached with the love of Christ is real.

PURPOSE

Writing from prison and awaiting execution, Paul seeks to impart his final words of wisdom to his spiritual son Timothy. He carries some of the concerns over from his first letter, such as dealing with false teachers. In this letter, however, Paul weaves together the themes of suffering, perseverance, and vindication in relation to his own experience and Christ's. Paul gives Timothy this example to encourage him in his own ministry, and also his Christian life.

AUTHOR AND AUDIENCE

Written in AD 65 shortly before his martyrdom at the order of the Roman Emperor Nero, Paul wants to make sure Timothy is instructed about serving the church as God's man. There is a spiritual inheritance found in 2 Timothy for every true minister of the gospel and for every lover of God.

Many have recognized this letter as the most personal and heartfelt of all of Paul's writings. He names twenty-three individuals—both friends and foes. He opens his heart and gives intimate details of his life, and he shares his desire to see Timothy advance in his calling.

Apparently, Timothy is still in Ephesus fulfilling the mandate Paul gave him in his first letter. Paul writes to his spiritual son knowing that death is near. He longed to see Timothy again and desired to make sure he was encouraged to finish his race to the end.

MAJOR THEMES

False Teachers and Doctrine. Apparently the same situation of unorthodox teaching Paul addressed in his first letter was still a problem. This time Paul calls these false teachers out by name: Hymenaeus and Philetus "are like gangrene," he says, who "have already spread their poison to many" (2:17). He urges Timothy to unapologetically preach the Word of Truth and stay away from their foolish arguments.

Suffering and Perseverance. From a Roman prison, waiting to be executed, Paul urges his gospel coworker to suffer as he has for the gospel. Paul calls Timothy into such living not only because of his own willingness to suffer but also because of Christ's own experience of death. He drives home this calling for courage by offering shameful examples of believers who've betrayed such a calling. Instead, Timothy—and we—are called to persevere through suffering like Paul, and like Christ, in order to receive their reward.

Faithfulness in Life and Ministry. As you might expect from a last will and testament, Paul instructs Timothy to pick up where he left off by carrying out his ministry with dedication and faithfully preaching the apostolic message. Paul offers his own life as an example of the kind of faithfulness to ministry and godliness he is urging Timothy to follow.

HOW TO READ & ENJOY

Titus

AUTHOR:
The apostle Paul

AUDIENCE:
Titus, Paul's "true son"

DATE:
AD 57, possibly 62–63

TYPE OF LITERATURE:
A letter

MAJOR THEMES:
Salvation, church leadership, and right living

OUTLINE:
- Letter Opening — 1:1–4
- Instructions to Titus — 1:5–16
- Instructions for Godly Living — 2:1–3:11
- Letter Closing — 3:12–15

ABOUT TITUS

Who was this friend of Paul named Titus? He was a Greek convert from Antioch and an apostolic church planter, much like Timothy, his peer. Paul describes him as a "true son" (1:4). He was likely a convert of Paul's ministry during his visit to Cyprus. Legend has it that Titus was a poet and a student of Greek philosophy when he had a prophetic dream that led him to study the Word of God and to become a Christ-follower. As God's faithful servant he traveled with Paul on his third missionary journey (2 Cor. 2:12–13; 7:5–15; 8:6–24). Paul commends him for his love, for his steadfast faith, and for bringing comfort to God's people.

After leaving Timothy in Ephesus, Paul accompanied Titus to Crete and left him there to establish the young church and set things in order. Believers who had been in the upper room had returned to Crete (Acts 2:11) and were in need of guidance and leadership from Titus.

Some say Paul wrote his letter to Titus as early as AD 57 from Nicopolis, prior to writing 2 Timothy. Others assume that he wrote this letter around the same time as he wrote his first letter to another young leader, Timothy, around 62–63.

Titus is one of three letters commonly known as the Pastoral Epistles, which also include 1 and 2 Timothy. Paul wrote them as an older apostle to his younger colleagues, Timothy and Titus, to encourage their ministries among God's people and to give further instructions to the churches he had planted.

The theme of Titus is that right living will always accompany right doctrine. Good words will flow from a solid understanding of God's Word. In today's culture, it is easy to say that we follow Christ, but our faith in him will be demonstrated by godly living. An understanding of truth will bring a demonstration of purity through our lives. God's saving grace is the same grace that empowers us to live for him.

The book of Titus reminds us that right beliefs should impact every area of our lives: family, relationships, work, and community.

PURPOSE

Like his letters to Timothy, Paul wrote this letter to Titus in order to give him instructions for building churches and raising up leaders. It was to be considered as a church-planting manual, helping this young apostle to encourage godly living and to establish godly churches.

It appears that Paul's first letter to Timothy and this one to Titus were both written around the same time, given the close parallels in the themes addressed. From church administration to confronting false teaching to maintaining the purity of personal conduct, Paul offered sage advice and pastoral wisdom to these young ministers. In the case of Titus, Paul wrote to address basic catechesis relevant to new believers, as well as the kinds of problems expected of a young church in a pagan culture. He also wrote his former companion to ask him to remain in Crete and care for the young church in Paul's absence, as well as to encourage the two companions accompanying the letter.

AUTHOR AND AUDIENCE

As with the two letters to Timothy, Paul's letter to Titus is a deeply personal one, for it was written from mentor to mentee—from an older, wiser, seasoned apostle to a younger, inexperienced minister. It's a letter between former colleagues on the frontline of missions, as Paul sought to give roots to the work they had started together by nurturing the community of believers through Titus's leadership.

Like Timothy, Paul had left Titus among his own ethnic people to continue the work they had started as a team; in this case, on the Greek island of Crete. As a convert of Paul, his "true son in the faith" (1:4), Titus became a trusted colleague in his gospel work. In fact, many believe the two made a missionary journey to Crete to evangelize the Greek island, occurring after the events of Acts 28 and before writing 2 Timothy, when Paul was imprisoned. As a young pastor stewarding a young church plant, Titus must have viewed Paul's letter as a welcomed breeze inflating the sails of his ministry!

MAJOR THEMES

Faith and Salvation in Jesus Christ. You would expect a letter from one ministry colleague to another to center on the good news of salvation in Christ. And Titus is indeed infused with it! After laboring alongside each other to proclaim the gospel, Paul recognized that their work was unfinished. He wanted Titus "to further the faith of God's chosen ones and lead them to the full knowledge of the truth that leads to godliness" (1:1) by discipling the young church in their shared salvation.

Part of how Paul emphasized this faith and salvation was by calling on Titus to appoint godly leaders to serve as examples to teach the faith, lead people to salvation, refute false teachings that destroy faith and distract from this salvation, and imitate the practical results of this faith: godly living resulting from salvation.

He also offered a basic catechism, or summary of primary Christian beliefs. He reminded them of the grace manifested in Jesus and the salvation he brought for all. He also reminded them of their previous fallen nature, how they "were easily led astray as slaves to worldly passions and pleasures" and "wasted [their] lives in doing evil" (3:3). And he shared with them a royal "hymn of salvation by grace," which declared the wonders of God's compassion, his overflowing love, and our new birth through our salvation by faith.

Appointing Church Leadership. The work of salvation among God's people and sharing the gospel within culture requires leaders who are of sound character and judgment. As he did with Timothy, Paul instructed Titus to appoint church leaders (elders or overseers) who were blameless, faithful in marriage and had well-behaved children, gentle and patient, and never drunk, violent, or greedy. They were to set an example for the rest of the community of believers in how they should live the truth of the gospel through godly living. They were also to firmly grasp the gospel message taught to them, in order to teach other believers the essential truths of the faith and how to respond to false teaching. This rubric for spirit-anointed leaders still serves as a trusted guide for church leadership.

Right Living for the Sake of the Gospel. Right living (orthopraxy) and right believing (orthodoxy) go hand in hand in Paul's letter to Titus. For when we believe in the gospel, and experience the joys of salvation, how else could we live other than in light of this mercy?

One thing Paul emphasizes, however, is that the gospel's grace actually trains us to live rightly. "This same grace," says Paul, "teaches us how to live each day as we turn our backs on ungodliness and indulgent lifestyles, and it equips us to live self-controlled, upright, godly lives in this present age" (2:12). Paul also emphasizes the need for godly men and women within the church to come alongside others to teach them to live rightly. May our right believing never excuse wrong living. And may our right living be evidence of our right believing.

HOW TO READ & ENJOY

Philemon

AUTHOR:
The apostle Paul

AUDIENCE:
Philemon, a slave owner

DATE:
AD 60–61

TYPE OF LITERATURE:
A letter

MAJOR THEMES:
Christian love, Christian belonging, fellowship, and slavery

OUTLINE:
- Letter Opening — 1–3
- Paul's Appreciation for Philemon — 4–7
- Paul's Appeal on Behalf of Onesimus — 8–21
- Letter Closing — 22–25

ABOUT PHILEMON

Paul's letter to Philemon is perhaps one of the most fascinating portions of our New Testament. It is a letter written with one purpose—to bring reconciliation between two brothers in Christ. It is a letter that promotes forgiveness as the key to unity and reconciliation. Everyone has experienced being offended, and everyone has offended another person. Yet in Christ, there is enough love to cover all sin and enough forgiveness to reconcile with those who have hurt or wounded us.

Here's the backstory of this intriguing letter: Philemon had been one of Paul's numerous coworkers in ministry. There was much history between Paul and Philemon, a person Paul considered a dear and trusted friend. It is believed that Philemon was wealthy and, along with his wife, led a dynamic house church in the city of Colossae, a city in Asia Minor (modern-day Turkey). Although Paul had never visited Colossae, there remained a strong bond of friendship between Philemon and Paul.

Apparently, Philemon owned a slave who stole from him and ran away. His name was Onesimus. (Onesimus means "useful" or "valuable." See Col. 4:9. This reference of Onesimus in Colossians suggests that Colossians was written shortly after Philemon.) By events that only God could orchestrate, the fugitive Onesimus found himself imprisoned next to Paul. Through the ministry of the Holy Spirit, Paul led his fellow prisoner to the Lord.

Paul sent the runaway slave back to Philemon carrying this letter in his hand asking his former master to fully receive Onesimus and be restored to him as a fellow believer. A slave who ran away could be punished by death according to the Roman laws of this era, yet Paul not only said Philemon should forgive him, but also love him as a brother returning home. This made-for-a-movie plot is contained in this very short letter you are about to read.

Orthodox Church tradition tells us that Onesimus served Christ faithfully throughout his life and became the bishop of the church of Ephesus after Timothy's death. The slave-turned-bishop was later taken once again as a prisoner to Rome where he testified before his judge Tertylus. He was condemned to death by stoning, and afterwards his corpse was beheaded in AD 109.

We should be grateful to God for gifting us this letter, because the dignity of every human being is brought forth powerfully in the story of Philemon and Onesimus—a story of forgiving love!

PURPOSE

The apostle Paul wrote his friend Philemon, a slave owner, mainly to encourage him to forgive and restore his slave Onesimus—and to do so no longer as a slave but as a brother in Christ. The theme of the book of Philemon is forgiving love.

Love forgives, restores, covers sin, and heals broken relationships. The sweetness of reconciliation is an incomparable joy. Only the love of Christ has the power to perform such a glorious restoration of relationships. We can thank God that he has given us this amazing letter to bring hope that forgiveness is waiting—waiting for all of us to experience for ourselves.

AUTHOR AND AUDIENCE

While a prisoner for the sake of the gospel, the apostle Paul wrote to a slave owner named Philemon. Although four names are listed in the letter's opening, it was customary in ancient letters to list the primary addressee first. It is clear throughout the main body of the letter that Paul singled out a single individual in his appeal: Philemon. This letter was a precious piece of correspondence between brothers bound by Christian love.

And yet it wasn't entirely private, for two other names and "the church" were also included, revealing the important bond between brothers and sisters in their activities through their common faith in Christ. This letter becomes a window into the heart of God for Christ's community, urging generous forgiving love.

MAJOR THEMES

Christian Belonging in a Common Faith. Mentioning Apphia and Archippus, as well as Philemon's house church, turned what might have been a private conversation into a public appeal. Though Paul may have been seeking to exert some sort of social pressure on Philemon, one of the enduring, relevant teachings of this letter is that our private business is a matter for the believing community since we belong to one another in a common faith.

Paul's use of *koinōnia* (Gr. for "fellowship") in v. 6 captures this reality. When people commit themselves to Christ, they are also committing themselves to a community. They bind themselves and become identified with one another so that they receive both the benefits and responsibilities of that "belonging." Paul invited Philemon and Onesimus, in addition to the house church, to think through the radical implications of their belonging to one another as slave and master, as well as a believing community.

The Love of Christ Performed. It is clear from Paul's entire work, as well as the general tone of this letter, that his appeal was rooted in the love of Christ. Paul wanted Philemon to respond to Onesimus in forgiveness and restoration in the same way Christ has responded to us. The manner in which Paul wrote his appeal and advocated for Onesimus—his tone and tenor, his words and arguments—also reflected the tender love of Christ.

We perform the same love that Christ himself performed. Paul performed Christ's love when he advocated for Onesimus, and in the way he appealed to Philemon. And he wanted Philemon to follow his performance with his slave-turned-brother.

Slavery and Brotherhood. There's an obvious facet to the relationship between Philemon and Onesimus: slavery. To our modern ears we think of the antebellum South and the injustices of the eighteenth and nineteenth centuries. Yet slavery looked quite different in the first century, so Paul wouldn't have necessarily viewed it as sinister, and he didn't seem to offer a treatise on abolitionism in his letter.

Still Paul is clearly interested that "we no longer see each other in our former state—Jew or non-Jew, [enslaved or free] . . . because we're all one through our union with Jesus Christ with no distinction between us" (Gal. 3:28). He wanted Philemon to reflect this common union in how he treated Onesimus: "welcome him no longer as a slave, but more than that, as a dearly loved brother" (v. 16). Onesimus had gone from being a valuable slave to a valuable brother in Christ (vv. 10–11).

This letter, then, seems to be less about slavery and more about the relationship between a slave and his master, now brothers in the Lord, both of whom Paul wants to experience forgiving love.

HOW TO READ & ENJOY

Hebrews

AUTHOR:
Unknown, but possibly Paul, Barnabas, Apollos, or Priscilla

AUDIENCE:
Christians converted from Judaism

DATE:
AD 50–64

TYPE OF LITERATURE:
A sermon in the form of a letter

MAJOR THEMES:
Jesus, the Old Testament, faith, perseverance, and heaven

OUTLINE:
- Prologue — 1:1–3
- Jesus' Superiority over Angels and Moses — 1:4–4:13
- Jesus' Superior Priesthood — 4:14–7:28
- Jesus' Superior Sacrifice and Covenant — 8:1–10:18
- A Call to Persevere — 10:19–12:29
- Final Instructions and Greetings — 13:1–25

ABOUT HEBREWS

The book of Hebrews presents the magnificent Jesus on every page!

The light of the Messiah brings truth out from the shadows and it shines brightly for all to see. Hebrews is written for every believer today, for we have crossed over from darkness to light and from doubt to faith. The name Hebrews means, "those who crossed over." We have passed from shadows to substance and from doubt to the reality of faith. What once was a symbol has now become substance, for all the pictures of the Old Testament have found their fulfillment in Jesus.

Hebrews takes us into the holy of holies as we come to him as priests, lovers, and worshipers. You will never be the same again when you absorb the light of God that shines from every chapter.

Jesus is the theme of Hebrews. You must learn from him and draw closer to him in order to understand the depth of this book, for Jesus is the language of God! When God now speaks to us, he speaks in the vocabulary of Jesus Christ. All of the Bible points to him. Can we truly understand the Bible if we don't come to him?

Hebrews is a divinely inspired composition given to show us the magnificence of Jesus as our glorious High Priest. He is greater than the law, the angels, the system of temple worship, and greater than any high priest or religious structure. Because our royal Priest gave his sacred blood for us, we now have unrestricted access to the holiest place of all. With no veil and nothing hindering our intimacy with God, we can come with an unbelievable boldness to his mercy-throne where we encounter enough grace to empower us through every difficulty. We find our true life in his presence.

Heaven's words are now before you, so read them with spiritual hunger and a passion to embrace truth, and live them out by the grace of Jesus, our Messiah.

God will help you!

PURPOSE

The purpose of the pastor's sermon is evident the further you read his letter: he is trying to prevent those he's addressing from abandoning their Christian faith and returning to Judaism. Along the way, the author teaches them—and us—about the superiority of Christ above the religious institutions of Moses and the Old Testament. The sermon-letter is filled with references to the old sacrificial system and priesthood of ancient Israel and explains how Jesus' death has replaced this old religious system—making it the perfect book to understand how Jesus' story fulfills Israel's story!

AUTHOR AND AUDIENCE

The book of Hebrews was most likely written sometime around AD 50–64. It had to have been written prior to Clement of Rome citing it as inspired (AD 95) and before the Roman war that destroyed the temple in AD 67–70. Though Hebrew's true authorship is unknown, the earliest church fathers taught that Hebrews was written in Hebrew by Paul for the Jewish people. Eusebius (AD 260–339) refers to an even earlier apostolic father, Clement of Alexandria (AD 150–211), who confirms without question that Paul wrote Hebrews in the Hebrew language for the Hebrew people. (See Eusebius, *History*, Book VI. XIV.) More recent scholarship, however, has begun to question this and speculate that it was written by Barnabas, Apollos, Priscilla, or another one of Paul's close associates.

Regardless of who wrote it, we are more certain about who read it—or rather, who first heard it read out loud, because Hebrews seems to be more of a sermon contained in a letter. The inscription placed on the original document is "To the Hebrews," and the major themes point to a group of Jewish Christians who may have been getting cold feet, wondering if they should return to Judaism. This sermon-letter is so steeped in ancient Jewish practices that it seems very likely the author is addressing Christians converted from Judaism. And yet, the letter still speaks to us today as those who enter into a better covenant by faith in Jesus Christ.

MAJOR THEMES

Christology: Christology is the study of the Christ, the Messiah, and this letter is a full-on course about our heavenly Savior! The revelation of Jesus fills the pages of Hebrews and it will set you free! He is our magnificent High Priest who is greater than Moses, greater than any sacrifice ever offered, greater than any prophet of old. He perfects our faith until we rise with him into the heavenly realm of priestly ministry. He warns us of turning back into ritual and religion, forgetting all the treasures of our faith. He stirs us to enter into the full rest by seeing Jesus alone as our perfection before the Father.

The Old Covenant Fulfilled: One of the central themes of Hebrews is the relationship of the new covenant established by the blood of Jesus, the Messiah to the old or "first covenant." Look at all the Old Testament imagery the pastor uses: Moses, the high priest, Melchizedek, the priestly order of Aaron, offerings and sacrifices, the ark of the covenant, and the Most Holy Place. Even though we are far removed from the original religious system of rules and rituals found in the Old Testament, we cannot afford to ignore the pastor's message: The high priesthood of Jesus is inherent to his identity as our all-sufficient Rescuer and Revealer!

The Reality of Heaven: The Hebrews sermon often speaks about heaven's reality. The pastor reveals it's the place where God keeps his throne; to be in heaven means to be in God's very presence; in it are the names of everyone whom God calls his own; and it is the place where our ultimate redemption and atonement took place. This last revelation of heaven is especially important, because Hebrews explains the old religious order of rules and rituals is no longer necessary because of the final sacrifice made for all people. All God commanded under the first covenant on earth became obsolete and disappeared thanks to what Jesus accomplished in heaven! The heavenly temple is where our ultimate salvation was accomplished, of which the earthly one could not.

Definition and Practice of Faith: Nowhere is there a better definition and explanation of faith in the New Testament than in the sermon-letter of Hebrews: "Now faith brings our hopes into reality and becomes the foundation needed to acquire the things we long for. It is all the evidence required to prove what is still unseen" (11:1). This is a far cry from the traditional understanding that faith is merely belief. Biblical faith claims a confidence beyond our own because it rests in the character of God, the foundation of our faith. Part of practicing faith is persevering in it. Despite the fact we live in a world that refuses to acknowledge God and opposes the church, we are called to persevere in our faith in him, just like the "great witnesses who encircle us like clouds" (12:1)! Hebrews warns against turning away in rebellion and unbelief, telling us the very divine message that saved us is the same one that will condemn us if we turn away.

HOW TO READ & ENJOY

James (Jacob)

AUTHOR:
Jacob, brother of Jesus

AUDIENCE:
Jewish Christians

DATE:
AD 45–47

TYPE OF LITERATURE:
A wisdom letter

MAJOR THEMES:
Wisdom, trials, the law, faith and works, poverty and wealth

OUTLINE:
- Greeting — 1:1
- Introducing the Three Themes: Wealth, Wisdom, Trials — 1:2–27
- Theme 1. Riches and Poverty — 2:1–26
- Theme 2: Wisdom and Speech — 3.1–4:12
- Theme 3: Trials and Temptation — 4:13–5:18
- Closing — 5:19–20

ABOUT JAMES (JACOB)

The Holy Spirit speaks through the Bible, God's Holy Word. His life-giving expression comes through each verse, and we are changed by receiving the Word of God. The book of James (Jacob) is rich with life-changing revelation, a feast to strengthen you and keep you on course. We thank God that this book is included in our Bibles for it gives us the understanding of the power of faith to produce good works. Faith works!

Actually, this letter is titled "Jacob." By calling this book James instead of Jacob the church loses a vital component of our Jewish beginnings. There is no "James" in Greek; it is Jacob. We would never say that God is the God of Abraham, Isaac, and James. Neither should we call this letter James, when it is in fact, the letter of Jacob!

Most scholars don't believe that he was a believer until after Jesus died and rose again (see John 7:5). Can you imagine growing up with the Son of God and not knowing it? Yet today many are able to see the works of Jesus all around them and still remain unconvinced. However, Jacob did become a powerful voice in the early church as the presiding apostle of the church of Jerusalem. And like his older brother, Jesus, he also was killed for his faith, in AD 62 according to the Jewish historian Josephus.

The book of Jacob and the book of Galatians are considered to be the first letters penned by the apostles most likely sometime between AD 45–47. So when we read this letter we are reading the earliest insights of the first generation of followers of Jesus who were mostly Jews.

Jacob gives us practical truths about what it means to be declared righteous by God. He gives us many clear insights on faith and walking in the truth. You might want to view this book as the New Testament version of Proverbs, for much of his writings speak of God's heavenly wisdom that can transform us.

PURPOSE

Although the book of Jacob is a letter, it reads more like a wisdom sermon addressing a number of crucial topics relevant to Jewish Christians using familiar language from the Old Testament. His letter was similar to so-called "diaspora letters" from ancient times written to the scattered Jewish people. Like those, it offers comfort and hope during persecution and trials, encourages faithful obedience to God, and provides spiritual instruction and encouragement on important matters relating to the unity and life of the church.

AUTHOR AND AUDIENCE

Although debated by some, it is believed that the Jacob who wrote this book (also known as James the Just) was the half brother of our Lord Jesus referred to in Galatians 1:19 and in Mark 6:3. This is amazing to think that the actual half brother of our Lord and Savior gives us truth to live by. We should listen to what Jacob has to say and take it to heart!

Given the dominant Jewish flavor of the letter, it appears he originally targeted Jewish Christians. Jacob (James) said, "I'm writing to all the twelve tribes of Israel who have been sown as seeds among the nations." His thoughts were meant to reach out to all the Christians who converted from Judaism who were scattered throughout the Roman Empire, calling their attention to the fulfillment of the promises for a Messiah in Jesus.

MAJOR THEMES

Wisdom from Above. The Greek word for wisdom, *sophia*, occurs four times in Jacob's (James') letter. His letter could be considered a wisdom sermon, for the style of the letter is similar to the Proverbs. Throughout his letter Jacob taps into the long tradition of Jewish wisdom and applies it to various practical topics for wise Christian living. He recognizes wisdom is necessary for trying circumstances; it involves insight into God's purposes and leads to spiritual maturity; and God is the source of all true wisdom.

Testing and Trials. In many ways, the wisdom letter of Jacob (James) is written to help guide those whose faith in God is being threatened by daily struggles and hardship. The kinds of testing and trials Jacob speaks of can range from religious persecution to financial difficulties, from health problems to even spiritual oppression. Jacob is clear such experiences are never a waste, there's a goal: Spiritual maturity born through perseverance.

The Law of Moses. While Jacob (James) doesn't directly refer to the law of the Old Testament, he does refer to "the royal law of love as given to us in this Scripture: 'You must love and value your neighbor' " (2:8). Of course Jesus Christ himself gave us this royal law, which he said summed up all the Law and Prophets. And for Jacob, anything that violates this law is as serious as violating any of the Ten Commandments. The law is relevant to Christian living not as legalistic rules and rituals, but as love of neighbor and God.

Faith and Good Deeds. One of the ongoing debates with Jacob's (James') letter is whether it contradicts the teachings of Paul and his theology of salvation by faith alone. While some of what Jacob says may seem like a contradiction, it isn't. Instead of undermining and opposing Paul's teaching that works cannot save, Jacob explains the kind of faith that does. "Faith that doesn't involve action is phony," Jacob argues. Faith that saves is a faith that works!

Poverty and Wealth. One of the major concerns of Jacob (James) seemed to be the huge gap between the rich and poor, even within the church. He encourages poor believers that they have been blessed with every privilege from God, though society may dismiss them. And to the rich he reminds them no amount of wealth from below could buy what they've been given from above. Jacob also writes against favoritism in the church of any kind, especially based on the size of one's pocketbook or the brand of their clothes.

HOW TO READ & ENJOY

1 Peter

AUTHOR:
The apostle Peter

AUDIENCE:
Churches in northwestern Asia Minor, modern-day Turkey

DATE:
AD 62–65

TYPE OF LITERATURE:
A letter

MAJOR THEMES:
God's nature, salvation, the church, the Christian life, and suffering

OUTLINE:
- Letter Opening — 1:1–2
- Identity as God's Chosen People and Foreigners — 1:3–2:10
- Living Honorably as Foreigners — 2:11–3:12
- Responding to Hostility as Foreigners — 3:13–4:6
- Living in Christian Solidarity as Foreigners — 4:7–19
- Suffering Together as Foreigners — 5:1–11
- Letter Closing — 5:12–14

ABOUT 1 PETER

Everyone needs grace to overcome life's hurdles. For some, they need to overcome a difficult marriage, or the frustration of children who have wandered away. For others it may be their limitations and hardships. First Peter is the book of strengthening grace and triumphant hope. There is an abundance of hopeful grace found within the verses of this book to set you free. You are a victorious overcomer, and God's grace is our fuel to empower our hearts to soar!

Peter was the first preacher to bring the gospel of Christ to the Jews in Jerusalem. At Pentecost he stood fearlessly and told the thousands gathered around him that they had denied the Holy One of God and crucified their Messiah. Yet just fifty days earlier, the apostle Peter, while Jesus was being tried by Pilate, denied that he even knew Jesus. Three times he succumbed to the weakness of his flesh. But Jesus had prophesied all this beforehand and gave him both a promise and a commission:

"I have prayed for you, Peter, that you would stay faithful to me no matter what comes. Remember this: after you have turned back to me and have been restored, make it your life mission to strengthen the faith of your brothers." (Luke 22:32)

Jesus told Peter that his life mission after his resurrection would be to strengthen the faith of believers worldwide. So you will discover that there is an unusual grace upon Peter's letters (known as part of the General Epistles) to strengthen you in your faith. Don't be surprised if after reading these letters you become emboldened to persevere, empowered to overcome, and encouraged to remain faithful to Christ. For the grace that restored Peter after his fall is also on Peter's letters to restore every believer and impart to them overcoming grace.

The Roman historian Eusebius informs us that Peter was crucified in Rome by Nero. The church tradition records that when Peter was being crucified, he pleaded with them to turn the cross upside down, stating that he was not worthy to be crucified in the same way as Jesus. Because of their respect for the godly Peter, the soldiers complied with his request. Peter turned the world upside down with the gospel power he carried, then he died on an upside-down cross. Peter experienced the triumph of grace. Our prayer for you is that the truth you read will release within you this same amazing grace and triumphant hope!

PURPOSE

There is rich teaching found in 1 Peter, showing us that the community of Christ is a holy nation made up of kings and priests and lovers of God. And Peter teaches us the ways of purity and righteousness, and how to remain faithful to God all the days of our lives as members of a kingdom that chafes against the values of the world. He wrote this letter to Christians undergoing persecution for living in a way that was different from their unbelieving neighbors. His letter was meant to encourage them in their suffering and give it purpose as a vital aspect of Christian living.

This is a letter about God and living for him—no matter what the costs. Some of the themes of 1 Peter include holiness and being faithful in the midst of persecution. When others turn away from us, the presence of Christ grows stronger in our lives. It pushes our souls deeper into God's overcoming grace. No matter what you face and no matter what you may be passing through in your life today, there is a power from on high to make you into an overcomer. Let Peter's letter show you the way!

AUTHOR AND AUDIENCE

Written about AD 62 from "Babylon" (a cryptic term for Rome), Peter longed to encourage and strengthen the faith of those who were being persecuted for following Christ. Although Aramaic was his first language, the fisherman Peter's refined use of Greek has caused some scholars to even doubt that he wrote this first epistle. We do know however that every good writer has a brilliant editor. Peter's editor for this letter was Silvanus (5:12), who no doubt helped Peter with the more elegant Greek words (much like the vocabulary of Paul), which are found in these five chapters.

Peter was the first missionary to go to the gentiles. After a divine trance he experienced on the rooftop in Joppa, Peter took the keys of the kingdom and opened the door of faith for the gentiles. He broke the religious limitation that the gospel was only meant for the Jews. Peter found his way to the house of Cornelius, a Roman gentile, and he and all his family became followers of Jesus. He continued this mission by writing to Christians living in the Roman regions of northeastern Asia Minor (modern-day Turkey), to encourage them in their suffering, provoke holy living and growth in God, and explain their new birth through Christ's blood. We all have a debt of love to the apostle Peter. Enjoy his letter as you read it with an open and thankful heart.

MAJOR THEMES

God the Father, God the Son, God the Holy Spirit. Who God is and what God is like is front and center in Peter's letter, because all of the teachings relate to him in some way. He's referred to as "Father God" or "God the Father," which should tell us something about how we encounter him: as a Father! He's also described as the mighty and powerful Creator and Judge, but also as our merciful and gracious Redeemer.

Of course as Redeemer, the Son of God is also featured prominently in this letter. One of the most important names Peter uses for Jesus is "Anointed One." This is a deeply Hebrew idea for the Messiah, the One whom God the Father destined "before the foundation of the earth was laid" (1:20) to be sacrificed for us "like a spotless, unblemished lamb" (1:19). It is this suffering that forms the basis for his saving work; our salvation was achieved through his crucifixion! While Jesus was fully revealed while he was on earth, he will be ultimately revealed on the last day, bringing with him the full revelation of our salvation and God's grace.

Then there is the Holy Spirit, who is vital for our ongoing Christian life, for a number of reasons: he's the One who has set us apart to be God's holy ones in the first place; he is the source of the gospel revelation, which goes out from us and draws people into God's family; and he lives in us to help us obey God as his chosen ones. Peter unveils before us the revelation-truth that he is our power as we live in this world as resident aliens and foreigners, awaiting Christ's return when he comes to make all things new.

The Nature of Our Salvation. Peter uses a number of images and words to convey to his readers the breadth and depth of their salvation in Jesus Christ. Followers of Christ have been "gloriously sprinkled with his blood" (1:2), have been redeemed once and for all through the precious blood of Christ (1:18–19), have been purified through obedience (1:22), have tasted "of the goodness of Yahweh and have experienced his kindness" (2:3), have been brought near to God (3:18).

This language reflects two ways in which believers have been changed: through Christ's sacrifice, and being born again. First, Peter uses sacrificial metaphors to explain what's happened to us. These are drawn from the ancient temple cultic practices of blood-shedding and purification. Second, Peter explains that our salvation is to be reborn into a new family, and we've inherited all of the benefits of that royal birth. So when we say we've been "born again," we are reflecting the language that Peter himself used to talk about what's happened to us!

Life in God's Family as a Spiritual "Nation." The inevitable outgrowth of our salvation and new birth in Christ is a new way of living and in concert with our new family and a spiritual "nation." We are to practice hope and holiness, fear of God, and growth in the knowledge of God. The reason why we devote ourselves to these pursuits is because we've been bought by the blood of Jesus. Without this new birth, there is no reason to obey; without the hope of salvation the Christian life is pointless.

What's interesting about Peter's letter is that he doesn't envision this kind of life as a solitary endeavor. Life in God's family is just that—a family affair! First, those in God's family are described as being "chosen" and "elect," which recalls the story of ancient Israel. This is intentional, as the church is the continuation and culmination of Israel as the new, true people of God. This idea of family frames the whole letter, appearing in the first verse and the last. They are the ones who've received God's grace and favor. It also frames how we are to live: we are to live as "obedient children" (1:14); we are to be holy as the Father is holy; we are to live within a new familial structure, accepting the authority of elders; and we are to love one another as siblings, wrapping ourselves with "the apron of a humble servant" (5:5).

Suffering and Persecution. Inevitably, when we live as obedient children of God, and the believing community takes seriously its role as "priests who are kings, a spiritual 'nation' set apart as God's devoted ones" (2:9), there's going to be conflict with the surrounding world. But Peter wants believers, who are "resident aliens and foreigners in this world" (2:11), to take heart: "the grief of many trials . . . reveal the sterling core of your faith" (1:6–7). Persecution is a refiner's fire

The New Testament **219**

that unfolds the brilliance of authentic faith. And when we do suffer for Christ, Jesus is praised, glorified, and honored. Ultimately, persecution is a privilege, for we "carry the Anointed One's name!" (4:16). God will never fail those who suffer for him!

HOW TO READ & ENJOY

2 Peter

AUTHOR:
The apostle Peter

AUDIENCE:
Churches in northwestern Asia Minor, modern-day Turkey

DATE:
AD 64–66

TYPE OF LITERATURE:
A letter

MAJOR THEMES:
God, humanity, salvation, ethics, eschatology, the church, and doctrine

OUTLINE:
- Letter Opening — 1:1–11
- Peter's Reason for Writing — 1:12–15
- Issue 1: The Power and Appearing of Our Lord — 1:16–18
- Issue 2: The Reliable and Valid Prophetic Message — 1:19–21
- Issue 3: False Teachers and Their Sure Destruction — 2:1–22
- Issue 4: The Delay and Destruction of the Lord's Day — 3:1–13
- Letter Closing — 3:14–18

ABOUT 2 PETER

God has given us a treasure through the writings of the fisherman turned apostle, Simon Peter. With descriptive terms, this tremendous man writes a letter that will guard our souls through the revelation of God's triumphant grace. Not long before Peter was martyred he took up the quill to write to those who shared with him the glorious hope of eternal life. Read these three chapters to learn, to grow, and to be warned. We can accept all that he tells us, for it is the Word of God.

Peter, the one who was asked three times, "Do you burn with love for me," has filled his letter with multiple references to love. It is the perfect expression of the life of Christ within every believer. Love triumphs over troubles and pain. It perseveres in the truth when false teaching surrounds us. A fiery, endless love for Christ is the antidote to stagnancy in our spiritual lives. Peter will not let you forget the importance of this love, especially when it comes to your growth in Christ.

Spiritual growth is a process of learning to love, so Peter speaks about growing in God's triumphant grace and becoming fully mature as those who share the divine nature with Christ (1:4). It begins with faith and virtue but it ends with love. Our diligence to hold to our faith will be rewarded in time with a greater love for God and for his people.

And finally, Peter brings the return of Christ to prominence. He speaks of the end of time and what will happen. He points us to the sure word of prophecy, rising like a daystar in our hearts, affirming within us that Christ is coming back. Be prepared to find ample reasons in 2 Peter for your faith to grow, even if it means enduring hardships. We thank God for the words Peter has left us—words that will never fade away.

PURPOSE

Peter writes as one who is facing imminent death. He describes being an eyewitness to the transfiguration of Christ. The two major themes of 2 Peter that outline his purpose for writing could be described as *truth triumphant* and *love unending*. It is necessary to address false teaching wherever it may be found. But have no fear, truth will triumph every time—especially when we speak the truth in love.

The burden that motivated Peter to write this letter seems to be the multiple false teachings that were beginning to threaten the health of the churches. Apparently, the false teachers taught the people that our freedom in Christ meant that sexual immorality was not an issue that should trouble us (2:14). They even made a mockery of the second coming of Christ (3:3–4). How we need Peter's wise exhortation today to stay pure until the coming of the Lord! As such, one could view 2 Peter as his farewell letter to the churches he loved, urging them to stay the course until Christ's coming.

AUTHOR AND AUDIENCE

Although the authorship of 2 Peter is the most contested of all the New Testament books in our Bible, there should be no doubt that the beloved Peter the "rock" is the human author of this inspired letter. In the third century Origen was the first of the church fathers to state that Peter was indeed the author, yet he did acknowledge that it was disputed by others. The stylistic differences are quite different between his first and second letter, but some scholars attribute this to a different amanuenses (secretary). Depending on the exact year Peter was martyred, we can approximate the date of writing this letter to AD 64–66.

It is believed that Peter was writing to churches within northwest Asia Minor, which is modern-day Turkey. These communities included the Roman regions of Pontus, Galatia, Cappadocia, Asia, and Bithynia. Based on the content of the letter and purpose that drove Peter to write it, a number of false teachers had begun influencing them in a moral direction that ran contrary to their calling as God's children in Christ. Peter was concerned they were vulnerable to these teachers. So he wrote to them as a pastor, to stimulate them to wholesome, Christ-centered thinking, believing, and living.

MAJOR THEMES

God the Father, God the Son, God the Holy Spirit. Unlike 1 Peter, God the Father is only mentioned a handful of times. Peter reveals he has created the cosmos and inspired the prophets; he is the ruler of angelic beings and human beings; the final judgment is described as "the coming of the day of God" (3:12), yet he is also patient and merciful. However, where God the Father was prominent in letter one, in letter two he is more in the background.

Not true of God the Son! Jesus is clearly in the foreground in Peter's second letter, yet in a way that's unique: Jesus is most often mentioned with a corresponding descriptive expression. He is "our God and Savior" (1:1); he is "our Lord" (1:2); he is "our Lord and Savior," as well as "the Messiah" (1:11); and he is described as "the Master," our sovereign Lord (2:1). He is the God-Savior, anointed by the Father, who reigns as supreme Lord.

Peter mentions the Holy Spirit only explicitly in 1:21, but he is also implied in 1:20. Though he occupies a small role in the letter, it isn't a minor one. For Peter's aim is to counter the false prophets affecting what these communities believed and how they lived. He wrote to remind the believers of their need to live a godly life and to confirm their calling. How are we to do that? We have "been given the prophetic word . . . reliable and fully validated" (1:19). And we can trust that message to guide our believing and behaving because those prophets were "inspired by the moving of the Holy Spirit" (1:21).

Entrapped Humanity and Divine Deliverance. Peter reveals something important about our human condition: humanity is entrapped by corrupt desires, and God's goodness has opened a way to escape that corruption through deliverance. First, Peter makes known in his letter the reality that the world is filled with "corrupt desires" (1:4). In fact, these desires are so powerful that they become entangled and defeated by them once again, to the point of turning their backs against "the sacred obligation that was given to them" in Christ (2:21).

And yet, Peter also makes known the revelation-truth that everything you need to "keep you from being inactive or fruitless in your pursuit of knowing Jesus Christ more intimately" and fully experiencing his deliverance has "already [been] planted deep within" (1:8). That's because through his divine initiative and by his divine power, God has called each of us by name and invited us to the rich experience of knowing Christ personally! For Peter, the idea of "knowing" is a crucial aspect of salvation. The Greek word *epignosis* carries with it the idea of acknowledging and recognizing Jesus as Lord and Savior, which leads to grace and peace, and the blossoming of Christian virtue.

Living in Light of the End. In 2 Peter, ethics (how we live) and eschatology (the end of the world) are intimately connected. In his final chapter, Peter draws our attention to the judgment that God will unfold on this reality, in preparation for a whole new one. But we aren't just waiting for the end; we're called to live in these "last days" in light of the end, the coming "day of God." Why? Because, as Peter reveals, in the end "every activity of man will be laid bare" (3:10). In light of this coming revelation and destruction he asks rhetorically, "don't you see how vital it is to live a holy life?" Which is why "We must be consumed with godliness" (3:11), and why he urges his readers to "be eager to be found living pure lives when you come into his presence, without blemish and filled with peace" (3:14).

False Teachers and False Teaching. One of the main reasons Peter wrote his letter was to urge the believing communities to guard against false teachers who would slip into their churches, secretly infiltrating them in order to divide and confuse them with destructive false teaching. Such people deny the sovereign Lord, live and teach immoral lifestyles, exploit true believers for their greedy gain, and pervert all kinds of Christian teachings and practices. While Peter does promise that "in their destruction they will be destroyed" (2:12), he also forewarns us not to be led astray by their lawlessness. Because for Peter, there is a very real threat of believers returning back to the very corrupt world system they escaped from in Christ! Peter believes right teachings are vital to the ongoing purity of the church and our individual godly lives.

HOW TO READ & ENJOY

1 John

AUTHOR:
The apostle John

AUDIENCE:
Communities in Asia Minor experiencing schisms

DATE:
AD 85

TYPE OF LITERATURE:
A letter

MAJOR THEMES:
Preserving truth, false teaching, God's character, Christ's centrality, and Christian discipleship

OUTLINE:
- Letter Opening — 1:1–4
- Walk in God's Light, Keep God's Commands — 1:5–2:11
- New Status, New Love — 2:12–17
- Believing and Living as God's Children — 2:18–3:24
- Test the Spirits — 4:1–6
- Love for Another, Love for God — 4:7–5:12
- Letter Closing — 5:13–21

ABOUT 1 JOHN

God is love! Let these words live within you! The glorious God of love is revealed in John's three letters. Written by the same John who penned his Gospel, the reader is taken into the Light of God. These beautiful words should be read over and over by every person on earth. God is love, and you can come to him by faith!

Everyone needs assurance from God that they are loved and cherished. The apostle John wrote this letter to assure us of the truths of God's love and mercy toward us. And when we receive his love, we are free to share it with others. As we love one another, we have the assurance that we are God's true spiritual children and that God's love is perfected in us. What joy John's words bring to our hearts!

Although the author is not named, it was clearly John the beloved who wrote this letter. (Only the New Testament books of Hebrews and 1 John do not directly name their authors.) He once walked on the shore of Lake Galilee—a fisherman, who left all to follow Jesus. And he taught all about life—eternal life, glorious life, abundant life! In Christ we find life, so John will always point us to Christ and our fellowship with him. In fact, John tells us four reasons why he wrote his letters: (1) to bring us into life-union (fellowship) with God (1 John 1:3); (2) that we might experience the fullness of joy (1 John 1:4); (3) that we might not sin (1 John 2:1); (4) that we might have the full assurance of our salvation (1 John 5:13).

The beloved apostle of Jesus reveals to us the revelation knowledge of who Jesus is and who we have become in him. John is the apostle of love. This letter is saturated with the love of God, which has been lavished upon us in Christ. And this love must be seen, made visible as we express his love toward one another. John reinforces this truth: we are to be ministers of love in how we walk in this life, demonstrating truth and kindness to all.

John's letter will bring a fresh understanding of God to your heart. Let him speak to you through his faithful servant John. Enjoy!

PURPOSE

John the beloved wrote his magisterial letter to bring the churches back into unity and clarity of faith, and beckon them to hold fast to the tradition and values they had already committed themselves to in Christ. There were false teachers who had come in and divided the flock with doctrines that diminished the glory of Christ. John's teachings always take us deeper into the truth and ways of God, and deeper into love for Jesus Christ. Anything that moves the heart away from loving Christ and loving others is to be viewed as suspect and diversionary. We can thank God for John's three letters to consistently point us back to the Light!

AUTHOR AND AUDIENCE

Although some contest it, there should be little doubt that the apostle John was responsible for writing this letter of passion, probably while he was in Ephesus around AD 85. The opening of the letter itself bears striking similarity to the Gospel that bears his name, extolling the Living Expression of God in almost poetic language. There are at least twelve other passages that have direct connection in both language, style, and scope with the fourth Gospel—showing that the beloved disciple of Jesus was the author of this beloved letter.

Unlike his other two letters, 1 John is not addressed to certain ones but to everyone. No particular audience is addressed in this letter, although there was a community over which John was an overseer in spiritual authority and fatherhood. Many believe John wrote this letter to clarify what he wrote earlier about the truth of Christ and to correct misinterpretations and misapplication of his testimony, especially by false teachers who had infiltrated this community. It was meant to encourage the believers who had been scattered by the Roman War of AD 67–70, and serve to encourage them in their understanding of their faith.

MAJOR THEMES

Preserving and Discerning Truth. In John's Gospel, he wrote his account of Jesus' life "so that you will fully believe that Jesus is the Anointed One, the Son of God" (20:31). He testified to the same truth in this letter so that those who believed wouldn't be led astray and would be "assured and know without a doubt that you have eternal life" (5:13). Such assurance and knowledge comes through the truth about Jesus, the Anointed One and Son of God, that John sought to preserve and help believers discern.

John was writing to a community troubled by false teachers who had distorted the truth of the gospel. For John, *truth* and *gospel* are equated, for the good news is about the one who was the Truth. So he defined a number of truths that one must believe in order to know eternal life, and encouraged ongoing discernment of the truth. Discernment is a major theme in this letter, and it is the task of the church to test the spirits, to "carefully examine what they say to determine if they are of God" (4:1).

Warning against Antichrists. John warns us that we must set our hearts firmly on the truths of Jesus Christ and his Word as protection from those whom John called *antichrists*. These people opposed the teachings of Christ, led people astray, and separated from the true community of Christ followers. John refuted antichrists in his day in a number of ways: he appealed to the teachings that had been with the church from the beginning, referenced early confessed creeds, pointed to the teachings and example of Jesus, appealed to the guidance of the Holy Spirit for all truth, and referenced our personal experience with God's heart through salvation. We guard against false teachers in these last days when we heed John's warnings and follow his guidance.

The Character of God. One of the more profound unveilings in 1 John is the character of God. Take a look at all we learn about him in John's Spirit-anointed letter: God is pure light, without a trace of darkness or impurity; faithfully forgives us of our sins, cleansing us from all unrighteousness; the essence of love, for he continually exists being love; the reality of all that is true; and the Father God who saves, having sent his Son into the world as its Savior. Ultimately, everything that is true about God is ours, because we have been born of God and enjoy unbroken fellowship with him.

The Centrality of Christ. It's only when we properly understand who Jesus Christ is that we can experience the heart of God. A distorted picture of Christ distorts how we live, which is why Christ takes center stage in John's letter. Every chapter is fixed on him: he is unveiled as the Living Expression of God; he is our atoning sacrifice, the one who shed his blood for our sins; he is our paraclete who advocates before the Father's throne on our behalf; he is our standard for living, the one in whom we are to actively remain; he will transform us into himself when he appears; he has come in real life flesh, not merely as a spirit-presence; and our new birth depends on believing in him, for he is the center of our believing as much as our faith.

Walking as Disciples of Christ. John's letter is largely concerned with preserving and discerning the truth about Jesus. Yet truth isn't only something to know in the head; it's something that we do with our whole self. John uses the metaphor of "walking" for the kind of life we're called to live—an image from the Hebrew Scriptures suggesting a manner and style of living that one is fully committed to. We are to walk in the pure light, not the realm of darkness; we are to walk in self-sacrificing love, not hate. Disciples of Christ walk the truth, which manifests itself as love. Of course, we know what love is because of Jesus: "This is how we have discovered love's reality: Jesus sacrificed his life for us" (3:16). John says the essence of our Christian life is emulating this love, which results in fellowship with God.

HOW TO READ & ENJY

2 John

AUTHOR:
The apostle John

AUDIENCE:
Communities in Asia Minor experiencing schisms

DATE:
AD 85–90

TYPE OF LITERATURE:
A letter

MAJOR THEMES:
Truth, brotherly love, and false teachers

OUTLINE:
Letter Opening — 1–3
An Exhortation to Walk in Truth and Love — 4–6
A Warning against False Teachers — 7–11
Letter Closing — 12–13

ABOUT 2 JOHN

The book of 2 John points us to the truth and encourages us to hold it fast and never let it go. The theme of John's second letter could be described as "loving truth." Truth generates love, and love will always be faithful to the truth. To love God is to love his truth and cherish it in our hearts.

   Some scholars believe that John penned what we've called his second letter actually first, before 1 John. Given that it addresses the same heartbreaking situation of schisms over false teaching that were wrecking the fragile churches under John's care in Asia Minor, some see this as a quick, almost hurriedly written note from the heart of a spiritual father to his children in trouble. Then he followed up his initial warnings with a second letter (which we know as 1 John) to make a greater appeal and guard their ongoing spiritual lives. Others see in this letter a follow-up to the first one, possibly written to a more distant audience, or even as a cover letter to 1 John given its personal greetings.

Regardless, what's evident is that John was deeply burdened about the chaos being caused in his network of churches. This beloved disciple of Jesus wanted his disciples to experience the pure love and truth that had already been birthed in their hearts. He also wanted them to walk in love, for to walk in love is to walk in the truth of God.

John's letter will bring a fresh understanding of God to your heart. Let him speak to you through his faithful servant John. Enjoy!

PURPOSE

As with his first letter, John wrote to the communities to which he was an overseer ("the elder" is a title suggesting spiritual authority) with one singular purpose: to guard and protect them from the false teachers who had gone among them and were deceiving them. These were itinerant teachers who were bearing a "truth" contrary to the received Spirit-anointed truth of the gospel. He writes as a spiritual father who was concerned about schisms wreaking havoc among his beloved children.

AUTHOR AND AUDIENCE

While the letter only identifies the author as "the elder," it's clear he was in a position of spiritual authority over his community and wrote in a similar manner and tone as both 1 John and the Gospel of John. Given this, it's no surprise that the tradition from the earliest days of the church assumed the apostle John authored the letter. Though the text doesn't bear his name, early leaders like Polycarp and Papias both ascribed it to him.

Possibly written earlier than his first letter, John addressed this one to the "chosen woman and her children." Most commentators see this as a metaphor for the church with its spiritual believers (children), believing that John the Elder wrote the letter to a church or network of churches. Some have viewed it more literally as written to an unnamed woman or a woman named Elekta or Kyria (feminine of *kurios*, "lord"). Regardless of who the letter was written to, it is inspired of God to bring truth to our hearts and keep us from evil.

MAJOR THEMES

Walking and Staying in the Truth. As with his first letter, John is concerned with the truth of the gospel—not only that believers guard it, but also walk in it and stay in it. The living truth of Christ has a permanent home in our lives, and will stay with us for all eternity. But we're also commanded to actively walk in the truth and stay in the truth—because as John says, "Anyone who wanders away and does not remain faithful to the teaching of Christ has no relationship with God" (9). For it's only when we continue in the truth that we have intimate connection with both the Father and the Son.

Loving One Another. Not only are we to love truth, we're to love each other. After all, this isn't a new command but one we've had from the beginning of time—and one our Lord and Savior Jesus Christ himself gave us. Loving one another means following the commands of Christ, which are always directed both upward (to God) and outward (to others). When we love our neighbor as ourselves, we are also loving the God who made them and saved them!

Warning about False Teachers. Finally, John warned against "deceivers" who might come into our midst and go beyond the teachings of Christ—trying to drag us with them. Early on, some believers thought this letter had either been a cover letter to 1 John, or an appendix added to its end. This makes sense given its close connection with John's first letter warning against false teachers. John reiterates our need to watch out for such antichrists—going so far as to instruct us not even to show hospitality to them, for anyone who welcomes them shares in their wicked work.

HOW TO READ & ENJOY

3 John

AUTHOR:
The apostle John

AUDIENCE:
Gaius, a friend of John

DATE:
AD 85–90

TYPE OF LITERATURE:
A letter

MAJOR THEMES:
Truth, hospitality, divisiveness, and doing good

OUTLINE:
- Letter Opening — 1–4
- An Exhortation to Show Hospitality — 5–8
- An Example of Inhospitality — 9–11
- Letter Closing — 12–15

ABOUT 3 JOHN

Though it is almost the smallest of the New Testament letters, this piece of ancient correspondence offers us a glimpse into a problem every modern church should consider: hospitality, especially for those called and anointed by Christ as ministers of his gospel.

There's a good chance that one of the characters in the letter, Demetrius, was himself a missionary who was associated with the apostle John and actually carried it as a sort of letter of introduction to the letter's recipient, Gaius. This dear man was known to John as a faithful host for missionaries who were spreading the gospel in the region. One can imagine Gaius rolling out the red carpet, breaking out the fine china, and making up an extra bed for Christ's emissaries who were tirelessly working on behalf of the Lord. Oh to be known for being a welcoming spirit, and for pouring out love and support for the sake of others! And woe to the one who denies hospitality and stirs up trouble within the body, which is exactly what one of the other characters had done.

John's motivation for penning and sending his letter to the small community in modern-day Turkey (Asia Minor) was to commend hospitality as a way of expressing Christian love. John was thrilled at how Gaius had welcomed traveling evangelists throughout the region, and he wanted him to continue this show of support. John's letter will bring a fresh understanding of God to your heart. Let him speak to you through his faithful servant John. Enjoy!

PURPOSE

John's third letter, similar in structure and vocabulary as his second letter, was more of a general letter sent to the churches scattered throughout Turkey (Asia Minor), even as it was addressed to one leader of one local community. John wrote to them to encourage them to welcome itinerant minsters who would travel and teach the different congregations—commending a particularly hospitable church leader, Gaius. He also warned against allowing pride and self-centeredness to get in the way of showing such love and support. It is a letter of hospitality and carries John's trademark truths of showing love and grace to all.

AUTHOR AND AUDIENCE

This intimate letter between Christian brothers addressing a situation in a local church involved four people: the elder, who sent the note; Gaius, who received the letter; and Diotrephes and Demetrius, church leaders in the region mentioned in the letter. Though various suggestions have been offered as to the identity of this elder, as with 2 John early Christians identified him as the apostle John, beloved disciple of Jesus. Although he wrote to one church leader in Asia Minor, the letter may have been intended for a wider audience to encourage them to continue to support missionaries bearing the gospel of Christ with open-armed hospitality.

MAJOR THEMES

Walking in the Truth. This is a common theme in John's letters, walking in the truth of Christ. Such walking is not only a joyful experience for those who are spiritually responsible for others (like parents when they see their children walking with Christ); it's also a joyful experience for believers, whose souls get along well in spiritual health as they maintain their commitment to Jesus in words and deeds.

Showing Christian Hospitality. True hospitality is a lost art in some churches today and must be valued. Gaius stands as an example to all of how it looks to faithfully demonstrate loving hospitality to our fellow brothers and sisters in Christ—especially when it comes to ministers of the gospel, who deserve our full, generous support. True Christian commitment to truth means a commitment to love through support.

Divisiveness within the Body. One of the greatest toxins to the body of Christ is divisiveness—whether that's a division in truth that false teachers bring, or a division in love that some believers create. Such an attitude manifests itself in pride, inhospitality, gossip, slander, malice, and obstruction. Not only did John warn against such people, he warned against imitating them within the body. We should name them and call such people out—just as John did with Diotrephes.

Doing and Imitating Good. "Don't imitate what is evil," John wrote, "but imitate that which is good" (11). John reveals something important about what we are to imitate: the *good* here is not just any good, but godly good. It's goodness reflecting God's good character and good acts, built on his inspiring love. Such people prove they are of God, and those who don't imitate good prove they've never been in relationship with him in the first place.

HOW TO READ & ENJOY

Jude (Judah)

AUTHOR:
The apostle Judah, also known as Jude

AUDIENCE:
Eastern Mediterranean Christians, all God's lovers

DATE:
AD 58–60

TYPE OF LITERATURE:
A letter

MAJOR THEMES:
Christian faith, Christian life, God's character, salvation, and judgment

OUTLINE:
- Letter Opening — 1–2
- Judah's Reason for Writing — 3
- Judah's Arguments against the False Teachers — 4–16
- Judah's Call to Persevere — 17–23
- Letter Closing — 24–25

ABOUT JUDE (JUDAH)

The name of this book from the Greek text is *Judas*, which is taken from the Hebrew/Aramaic name Judah. The actual name of this book is Judah! One of the most neglected letters in the New Testament, Judah carries a message for every believer today: there is a truth worth fighting for. It is not only written to you, as one who loves the truth; it is also entrusted to you—to preserve, defend, contend, and struggle for.

Though Judah wrote to a specific community who had been influenced by false teachers and foreign ideas to the gospel, his warning to persevere in both believing in our faith and living out our faith is timeless—for the church has always had to contend with false teachers who have tried to pervert the message of God's grace and distort the nature of our salvation.

The one striking fact you'll discover in reading Judah's letter is that he likely refers to two extrabiblical books, *The Assumption of Moses* (v. 9), and the *Book of 1 Enoch* (vv. 14–15). (Or "The Testament of Moses." Some scholars believe *The Assumption of Moses* and *The Testament of Moses* are one in the same. Others see them as different pseudegraphical books.) This has led some to reject Judah entirely, but there is no law against quoting from non-inspired books or borrowing thoughts and including them in an inspired text. They teach us some important revelation-truths about corruption and ungodliness.

By the last half of the first century there were already many false teachers who had infiltrated the ranks of the believers. Judah writes to warn and identify them as those who cause divisions and distort the truths of our faith. Yet you'll find some of the most beautiful treasures in his book, such as praying in the spirit, and the duty of keeping our hearts burning with passion for Jesus. Today, almost two thousand years after Judah wrote his short letter, we still need to guard our hearts and our churches from being led astray from the simplicity of the gospel. After all, these are truths worth fighting for!

PURPOSE

Judah's reason for writing his letter is clear: he needed to urge believers "to vigorously defend and contend for the beliefs that we cherish" (v. 3). Intruders had sown the seeds of false teaching among the believers, creating chaos and confusion. So Judah urged them to preserve, contend for, struggle for, and defend the body of truth we've received from the inspired Word of God, through the teaching ministry of the apostles.

Perhaps to combat and prevent the dangers of the sown heresy from fully blooming, Judah ended his letter by giving seven commands: (1) Keep building up your inner life on the foundation of faith. (2) Pray in the Holy Spirit. (3) Fasten your life to the love of God. (4) Receive more mercy from our Lord Jesus Christ. (5) Have compassion on the wavering. (6) Save the lost. (7) Hate any compromise that will stain our lives. It's when we live the truth of the gospel that we are sure to defend and contend for it most effectively.

AUTHOR AND AUDIENCE

Judah (Jude) is one of the two New Testament books written by half brothers of Jesus—Jacob and Judah. Judah was possibly the youngest of the four brothers of Jesus (Matt. 13:55). Many scholars believe that Judah may have written his letter only twenty to twenty-five years after the life and resurrection of Jesus (AD 58–60). Although the exact audience is unclear, he most likely was addressing believers who lived in a Greek-speaking area not far from Palestine in the eastern Mediterranean region, including Syria and Egypt. All we know is they had received the gospel from the apostles, and were being disrupted by outsiders who brought ideas foreign to that received teaching.

MAJOR THEMES

Defend and Contend for the Faith. Judah's message reminds us to defend and contend for the faith entrusted to us. It is clear that he is not speaking of faith as simply believing in God, but *the (Christian) faith*. This encompasses the body of truth we receive from the inspired Word of God, delivered by the apostles—the gospel. Judah used an athletic metaphor to drive home the point that we need to struggle as in a great contest, exerting great effort to promote the noble cause of the gospel's advance—while defending these core beliefs (transmitted through generations of Christians) from the threat of false teachers.

Live the Faith. Not only is Judah concerned about the content of the believer's faith, he's also concerned about its expression—for right beliefs and right living go hand-in-hand. The false teachers who had sneaked into the churches were teaching a faith that had "perverted the message of God's grace into a license to commit immorality" (v. 4). Judah feared this perverted message would destroy their beliefs, which would in turn cause them to live ungodly lives. After warning of such examples, he urged believers to live their faith through discipleship, prayer, remaining in God's love, accepting Christ's mercy, being compassionate, evangelistic, and with discernment. Living our faith by showing it is the surest way to preserve and contend for it!

The Character of God. Judah offers us a rich understanding of the character and person of God—beginning with the words "chosen," "wrapped in the love," and "kept and guarded." This is what God has done for us who have believed! He is also the God who reveals, for he has entrusted to us revelation-truths through his apostles, leading to our salvation. Then there are shades of the Trinity: he urges believers to pray in the Holy Spirit, remain in God's (the Father's) love, and receive the mercy of Jesus Christ (vv. 20–21). Finally, we find one of the most vibrant, almost hymnic descriptions of God at the end in vv. 24–25: God keeps us from sin, revealing us as faultless; is heralded as Savior; and possesses endless glory and majesty, power and authority.

Coming Salvation and Judgment. Judah had wanted to write to the believers "about our amazing salvation we all participate in" (v. 3) for that is what we possess right now! Yet we are also waiting for our final salvation when Christ comes bearing eternal life. This is why Judah's theme of defending and contending for the faith is so important, for we are to preserve and persevere in our salvation until the end. There's another reason: judgment. For along with his salvation, the Lord will bear judgment for all the ungodly. Judah reveals that God destroys those who are guilty of unbelief and who give themselves to immorality, slander heavenly beings, and corrupt his church. Judgment makes the issue of false teaching that much more important, for such people sow seeds of division and doubt. This is why we're called to come alongside those who doubt their salvation and offer Christ's saving work in order to snatch people from the fires of judgment.

HOW TO READ & ENJOY

Revelation

AUTHOR:
The apostle John

AUDIENCE:
Every church and believer in every age

DATE:
AD 64–68 or 92–95

TYPE OF LITERATURE:
Prophetic apocalyptic literature

MAJOR THEMES:
Spiritual symbols, Jesus Christ, the church, perseverance, judgment and destruction, rescue and re-creation

OUTLINE:
- Introduction — 1:1–20
- Christ's Letters to the Churches — 2:1–3:22
- John's Vision of God's Throne Room — 4:1–5:14
- The Lamb Opens the Sealed Scrolls — 6:1–8:5
- Seven Angels Sound the Trumpets — 8:6–11:19
- God Fights the Forces of Evil — 12:1–15:4
- Seven Angels Bring the Seven Last Plagues — 15:5–16:21
- Judgment and Destruction, Rejoicing and Reign — 17:1–20:15
- A New Heaven, a New Earth, the New Jerusalem — 21:1–22:5
- Conclusion — 22:6–21

ABOUT REVELATION

Do you long for the fullness of Christ and desire to know him intimately as a friend? Do you want more than anything else to be consumed with the glory of Jesus Christ? All this and more is waiting for you to discover in the pages of the book of Revelation!

The most deeply spiritual book of the New Testament is before you now. Revelation is a book written to satisfy your craving to be one with Jesus Christ. It is something that must be "eaten" (Rev. 10:9) if it is to be understood. It has the power to profoundly change a generation who gives heed to what has been written.

Of all the sixty-six books that comprise our Bible, the last book is meant to thrill and exhilarate the believer. A beautiful Christ is unveiled, and an overcoming company of saints is seen rising into his fullness. The book of Revelation is exciting, powerful, dynamic, and more than meets the eye. It can be more to us than merely an unveiling of events to come; it can be an experience of encountering Christ. Revelation is a glory book and requires a glory heart to receive it.

God is ready to unveil this book to those who are ready to embrace it, eat it, and live fully in the splendor of Christ. This is more than a vision given to John; it is meant to be an inward discovery, a delightful unveiling within us. This is not a drama of Satan's worst, but a supernatural drama of God's best, pouring through his beautiful Son, Jesus Christ.

Revelation is the unique deposit of the fullness of every truth in the Scriptures wrapped up in the person and glory of Jesus Christ. Genesis is the book of beginnings. Revelation is the book of consummation. All things are made new as we are given a new name (nature), a new song (message), a New Jerusalem (a realm of union with God), a new heaven (government), and a new earth (order, expression). The Bible ends with the passing away of all that is old and the establishment of all that is new. These symbols of deeper realities require ears to hear and hearts to discern.

When Jesus unveiled the deep spiritual truths of the heart of God, he spoke in parables (Matt. 13:34), using symbols to teach us. In fact, when Jesus spoke clearly, his disciples were amazed (John 16:29). Today, he continues to teach us through the language of the heart—through pictures, parables, and allegories.

We must allow the Lord to transform our natural ears into spiritual ones if the truths of this book are to be heard and received in our spirits. Without a deep and abiding desire to see Christ, and not just have a preview of what's coming, we are all in the dark. The key that unlocks the book of Revelation is a passion to know Jesus Christ. To those who have this passion to know him, more will be given. Jesus is the only one worthy to open the seals of the book. And his Spirit is present today to break open those seals and bring deep understanding to our hearts.

God's glory is found when truth touches the heart and strikes us with light. Understanding comes when humility and revelation meet. As our hearts are touched by truth, our minds are filled with light. This revelation enabled Daniel to interpret dreams, Paul to teach heavenly truths, and John to write the Revelation. With unveiled faces we come to the well of the Word and drink deeply, not merely to seek answers, but to discover him.

May the Lord himself, who inspired John to write the Revelation, inspire your heart as you read it to love Jesus more. And may this book be more than a manual of coming events, but also an unveiling of the coming King!

PURPOSE

Why was the book of Revelation written? This is an important question given there have been multiple views on the book's purpose over the ages. Some view it as a fascinating piece of first-century writing with little or no relevance for us today. Others see Revelation as a code book describing a specific outline of history written in advance. Many have tried to decode the book from a historical perspective to find the major world events of the past two thousand years, or to prove that most of the book has already been fulfilled. Others interpret it as a handbook that predicts the cataclysmic events that will bring the nations to Armageddon and the end of the world.

But perhaps there is yet another viewpoint to guide us through this incredible book of mysteries. We must stop and allow the Holy Spirit to unveil its treasures to us. Only the Holy Spirit can unveil Christ to the unbeliever, and only the Holy Spirit can unveil the glory of Christ to those who know him. The purpose of the Revelation is to unveil Christ to our hearts like no other book in the Bible.

This is the book of Revelation, not the book of revelations (plural). It emphasizes one revelation alone: Christ unveiled to his people. To read this book with any other focus is to miss the center of its meaning. There are other truths waiting for us to discover, but only after centering our gaze on this one—our Magnificent Obsession.

AUTHOR AND AUDIENCE

It was to the "beloved" disciple, John, that this revelation was first imparted. John was the apostle of love. In his later years he taught us the importance of love, "for God is love" (1 John 4:8). John wrote for us an incredible book full of symbols and intriguing insights into the heart of God. It takes us behind the veil into the holy of holies. It spills forth with puzzling information about the mark of the beast, Armageddon, the four horsemen, Babylon the great, and a woman clothed with the sun. Through the ages the images found in this book—images of terror and catastrophe—have significantly influenced the thinking of millions of Christians. Yet despite nearly two thousand years of fascination with this book, the meaning of John's masterpiece continues to be debated.

It is generally believed that this book was written during two possible periods: between AD 64–68 under the reign of Emperor Nero, and during his persecution and terror; or between AD 92–95 under the reign of Emperor Domitian, who similarly launched a campaign of persecution to destroy the church. Regardless of when it was written, what's more important is to whom this letter was written: Revelation was written for every church, every lover of God in every generation. It is for *today*! It is for *you* to understand and embrace as much as it was for the early churches who received John's letter of Christ's unveiling.

INTERPRETING THE BOOK OF REVELATION

There are levels to understanding God's Word. When the transcendent, glorious God gives us an inspired book, it compels us to dig deeper and look beyond the cursory meaning of words. Yes, there is a plain and literal surface meaning to all that God has given us, but we know there is yet more to discover. The Bible is full of symbols, poetry, metaphors, and figurative language that engages our spirits, not merely our minds.

The prophetic writings of the Bible, including the book of Revelation, require that we look at them like gazing upon the finest piece of art. They beg us to ponder, to inquire, to study further until they yield their beauty and meaning. With eyes opened by the Holy Spirit we find a spiritual application to all that is written, for that is where we touch the reality of God through his Word.

As we grow up into more of Christ in all things, the Word of God will become richer and more delightful to our hearts. It will speak to us out of our relationship with Christ, for intimacy is always where revelation begins to come into our spirit.

Every commentator on the book of Revelation agrees that it is rooted in the symbolism of the Old Testament, as it is full of allusions to the prophetic writings of Scripture. Without understanding the other sixty-five books of the Bible, the last book becomes too mysterious and unknowable to the heart of man. Indeed, the mind of man is incapable of receiving the mysteries and ways of God. Revelation must come to our spirits before we can crack open the Revelation (unveiling) of Jesus Christ. The same Spirit who inspired the book will unveil the meaning of the book to those who trust him.

Several views have dominated how Christians have interpreted and understood the symbols of this divine unveiling over the generations, known in these ways: preterist, futurist, historicist, and idealist.

Preterist Re-viewing of History. This view insists that we look at most of the book (chs. 1–18) as having been already fulfilled early in the church's history. This means many of the symbols of this unveiling relate to the events of the first century instead of a future one. Those who hold this view believe Revelation addresses faithfulness to God in the face of pagan persecution, and offers hope for God's ultimate, eventual victory.

Futurist Pre-viewing of History. This view goes in the other direction: it interprets the events as largely happening in the future. The symbols are prophetic pointers to the end of the world, previewing what will take place leading up to the return of Christ. Rather than having relevance strictly to first-century believers, it offers believers in every age assurance of evil's destruction and ultimate rescue.

Song of Songs **245**

Historicist Identifying of History. This approach sees John's Revelation as identifying the major movements of church history, and then reading them back into the symbols and prophecies of the book. Some also consider how current events fulfill New Testament apocalyptic symbolism. A prime example is identifying the Beast with various dictators through history, like Napoleon or Hitler or Saddam Hussein. The seals, trumpets, bowls, and plagues are identified as being a series of successive events, with the hope of Christ's return being very near.

Idealist Symbolizing of History. This model of interpretation finds significance in the symbols of deeper meaning embedded throughout Revelation for the church between Christ's first and second comings. These symbols offer every church and believer in every age timeless spiritual truths unrelated to specific historical events. It is concerned with the battle between good and evil, and between the church and the world at all periods in Christian history, depicting the continuous victory of believers and Christ.

This translation of Revelation agrees with many interpreters that all of these models have validity; measures of truth get unlocked by each one. Yet as you read through the Bible, you will find time after time that symbols, parables, and pictures are the true language of God, imparting revelation-truth regardless of historical periods of circumstances. The same is true for Revelation. In it we must look for the prophetic images and ask for an understanding of the spiritual viewpoints that help believers be overcomers today.

We can read the book of Revelation as a preterist re-viewing of human history, as a futurist pre-viewing of what is to come, and also as a dynamic super-viewing of the unveiling of Christ in his people. The Revelation of Jesus Christ is something that is unveiled *in* us, not just to us. Christ in us is our hope of glory. We must see the indwelling Christ within us as the hope that moves us into fullness and expectancy. Christ is the hope of God expressing himself through us to all his creation, which is groaning and waiting for the "unveiling" of the sons of God. (The same Greek word used in Rom. 8:19–20 is also found in the title of the last book of Scripture, the "Unveiling of Jesus Christ.")

MAJOR TOPICS

The Spiritual Language of Symbols. To discover all of God within his written Word is to learn the language of symbols. How much we miss when we ignore the poetic symbolism of the Bible! The Scriptures are full of symbols, such as wheat, tares, pearls, doors, veils, along with numbers, dimensions, and colors. God's language includes pictures and symbols, which point us to a greater reality. God will hide levels of truth from superficial seekers until we become those who hunger and thirst for true treasure—the revelation of God.

Revelation is not something that can be described; it must be *discovered*. God delights when he sees us seeking with all our hearts. We become like kings in his eyes, for "God conceals the revelation of his Word in the hiding place of his glory. But the honor of kings is revealed by how they thoroughly search out the deeper meaning of all that God says" (Prov. 25:2). God's glory is found in how he hides the treasure of his Word. Our glory is seen in how we seek it out.

Those who did not love our Lord Jesus when he walked the earth were blinded to who he was and to what he taught. They consistently misinterpreted his words. When he said, "After you've destroyed this temple, I will raise it up again in three days" (John 2:19), he caused a major controversy, all because they thought he was speaking literally. Yet we know he was speaking of the temple of his physical body. This controversy remained with him throughout the rest of his life and ministry. In fact, one of the issues that led to his crucifixion was his spiritualizing the meaning of the temple (see Mark 14:58). This misunderstanding was hurled at Jesus by the jeering crowd who watched his torturous death on the cross (see Matt. 27:39–40). It would be a mistake to miss truth because of a refusal to interpret some Scripture symbolically.

Another instance of this would be when Jesus spoke of eating his flesh and drinking his blood (see John 6:53). No one today would consider these words to be literal. We know the spiritual meaning of the text is to feast upon the sacrifice of Christ and commune with him through his Word, his blood, and his Spirit. Indeed, if we view the Bible as a spiritual book, yet refuse to look for the deep spiritual meaning in the text, we are closing our eyes to reality. The Word of God is a spiritual book that will feed our spirits, for the words he speaks into our hearts are truly *spirit* and *life* (see John 6:63)!

Jesus Christ Unveiled. We have in the Gospels the glorious story of our Lord Jesus as he walked this earth. We see his marvelous ministry of teaching, healing, delivering, and loving all. He was veiled in weak flesh, humiliated by others, and rejected. The last view we have of him in the Gospels is the resurrected Jesus ascending to heaven surrounded with clouds. But what happened after that? What is he like now? We need our eyes unveiled to see him as he now is. What you read in this book will present him in his present glory.

Some have described the book of Revelation as "the sixth gospel." We have the four Gospels in the beginning of our New Testament, and with the book of Acts we find the "fifth gospel," which demonstrates the power of the resurrected Jesus working through those who follow him. And in the last book of the Bible we discover the "sixth gospel," with yet another view of Jesus as the ascended, glorified God-Man who is unveiled before our eyes as Prophet, Priest, and King of kings.

As the Prophet, Jesus is the Faithful Witness who only speaks the Father's words. As the High Priest, Jesus is the Firstborn from the dead, who intercedes for us and releases mighty power to us. And as the King, Jesus is the Ruler of the kings of the earth. Each of these clues into his identity show forth his authority. Through the victory of Christ's death and resurrection he now holds the keys of death and the unseen world. There is nothing to fear, for he holds all authority (the keys). He rides forth to conquer everything within us that hinders the life of Christ emerging in our transformation. All the universe will one day be conquered by the One riding this white horse!

Jesus' Church Unveiled. The unveiling of Jesus Christ will also be our "unveiling" as those who believe in him, for we are his body on the earth. To receive a revelation of Christ, the head of the body, is to receive the revelation of the members of his body, the radiant ones who follow him. Christ is unveiled in heaven, and he is unveiled in his body. When he is unveiled, we are unveiled, for we are one with him in his glory (see Eph. 1:23; Col. 3:4).

Christ's letter to the churches imparts especially important revelation-truths to every believer, for he calls us to burn with light as his lampstands—a powerful metaphor for bringing illumination to the world as witnesses for God. This revelation also shows forth the church as God's temple, his dwelling place. And as Jesus' lovely bride, our co-reign with him has already begun where we are commissioned to do greater works of Jesus and spread the brilliance of his glory throughout the earth. Though the powers of the Abyss may come against us, we can be sure Jesus cares for both his church and its leaders, who are intimately bound to him.

The Judgment and Destruction of Old Order. From the opening of the first of the seven seals, many have understood the revelation-truth unveiled in this book as showing forth the earth's destruction. And yet, while traditionally this destruction has been taken literally, we understand it must also be taken symbolically. The old order of the natural realm is passing away and a new order is being established. Progressively, the superior light of the kingdom of God will make dim the light of the old.

The judgment of John's Revelation, another major theme alongside destruction, is also often misunderstood. For the anger and wrath of the Lamb is corrective and redemptive—not beastly rage, but fiery passion to judge whatever gets in the way between the Lamb and his bride. Further, we find the winds of judgment are being held back until the sons of God have the thoughts and mind of Christ. We are "sealed," which means we are protected from judgment. In Revelation, an angel carries the seal of the living God, speaking powerfully of God's grace and mercy, which will always triumph over judgment.

And yet, in the end, the world will experience a final judgment—where everything and everyone destructive to God's wonderful world will be cast into the lake of fire. Until then, we now enforce the judgment that took place on Calvary, where Satan was bound through Christ's death and resurrection. During the "thousand years" in which we live (since the death and resurrection of Jesus; see Rev. 20:2) we are given the authority to bind the strongman (Satan) and plunder his goods until evil is eventually and decisively destroyed.

The Rescue and Renewal of the Lamb. The end of the world as we know it isn't ultimately about judgment and destruction. It's about rescue and renewal, for the Lamb of God has won, and so have we! Though we have to pass through tribulation to enter the kingdom of God, we do so through the blood of Christ, knowing that our victory is sure. This unveiling shows the ultimate vindication of the people of God: we experience salvation from sin and death; we inherit the Holy City and its fount of living water.

One of the primary characteristics of prophetic apocalyptic writing is the exhortation to persevere. Endurance and faithfulness, conquering and obedience are all hallmarks of John's Revelation. It is the one who is victorious over the "beast" of the self-life who finds ultimate rescue and renewal. This isn't salvation by works. Rather, as we overcome by the power of the cross and take on the life of Christ for ourselves, we qualify as overcomers who sing the sacred song of Moses (15:3–4), sung as our final victory song.

Ultimately, as the Lord of Glory, Jesus is the bright Morning Star who signals the end of night and the beginning of God's perfect day, the end of the old order dominated by our self-life and the beginning of God's brand new order of righteousness, peace, and pure love. And he is coming quickly to finally make everything new and fresh!

PART THREE
One-Year Bible *Reading Plan*

Traditional Reading Plan: pgs 252–257

Chronological Reading Plan: pgs 258–263

Traditional Reading Plan

JANUARY

DAY	NEW TESTAMENT	OLD TESTAMENT	DAY	NEW TESTAMENT	OLD TESTAMENT
1	Matt 1	Gen 1–2	17	Matt 12:9–32	Gen 35–36
2	Matt 2	Gen 3–5	18	Matt 12:33–50	Gen 37–38
3	Matt 3	Gen 6–7	19	Matt 13:1–23	Gen 39–40
4	Matt 4	Gen 8–10	20	Matt 13:24–46	Gen 41–42
5	Matt 5:1–20	Gen 11–12	21	Matt 13:47–58	Gen 43–44
6	Matt 5:21–48	Gen 13–15	22	Matt 14	Gen 45–46
7	Matt 6:1–15	Gen 16–18	23	Matt 15:1–20	Gen 47–48
8	Matt 6:16–34	Gen 19–20	24	Matt 15:21–39	Gen 49–50
9	Matt 7	Gen 21–22	25	Matt 16	Ex 1–3
10	Matt 8	Gen 23–24	26	Matt 17	Ex 4–5
11	Matt 9:1–17	Gen 25	27	Matt 18:1–14	Ex 6–7
12	Matt 9:18–38	Gen 26–27	28	Matt 18:15–35	Ex 8–9
13	Matt 10:1–15	Gen 28–29	29	Matt 19	Ex 10–12
14	Matt 10:16–42	Gen 30	30	Matt 20:1–16	Ex 13–14
15	Matt 11	Gen 31–32	31	Matt 20:17–34	Ex 15–16
16	Matt 12:1–8	Gen 33–34			

FEBRUARY

DAY	NEW TESTAMENT	OLD TESTAMENT	DAY	NEW TESTAMENT	OLD TESTAMENT
1	Matt 21:1–27	Ex 17–19	15	Matt 27:1–26	Lev 7–8
2	Matt 21:28–46	Ex 20–21	16	Matt 27:27–56	Lev 9–10
3	Matt 22:1–22	Ex 22–23	17	Matt 27:57–66	Lev 11–12
4	Matt 22:23–46	Ex 24–25	18	Matt 28	Lev 13
5	Matt 23:1–22	Ex 26–27	19	Mark 1:1–28	Lev 14–15
6	Matt 23:23–39	Ex 28–29	20	Mark 1:29–45	Lev 16–17
7	Matt 24:1–28	Ex 30–31	21	Mark 2	Lev 18–19
8	Matt 24:29–51	Ex 32–33	22	Mark 3:1–19	Lev 20–22
9	Matt 25:1–13	Ex 34–35	23	Mark 3:20–35	Lev 23
10	Matt 25:14–46	Ex 36–37	24	Mark 4:1–25	Lev 24–25
11	Matt 26:1–13	Ex 38–39	25	Mark 4:26–41	Lev 26
12	Matt 26:14–35	Ex 40	26	Mark 5:1–20	Lev 27
13	Matt 26:36–56	Lev 1–4	27	Mark 5:21–43	Num 1–2
14	Matt 26:57–75	Lev 5–6	28	Mark 6:1–29	Num 3–4

How to Read Your Bible & Enjoy It!

Traditional Reading Plan

MARCH

DAY	NEW TESTAMENT	OLD TESTAMENT	DAY	NEW TESTAMENT	OLD TESTAMENT
1	Mark 6:30–56	Num 5–6	17	Mark 14:22–52	Num 34–35
2	Mark 7:1–23	Num 7	18	Mark 14:53–72	Num 36
3	Mark 7:24–37	Num 8	19	Mark 15:1–20	Deut 1–2
4	Mark 8:1–21	Num 9–10	20	Mark 15:21–47	Deut 3–4
5	Mark 8:22–38	Num 11–13	21	Mark 16	Deut 5–6
6	Mark 9:1–29	Num 14	22	Luke 1:1–25	Deut 7–9
7	Mark 9:30–50	Num 15–16	23	Luke 1:26–56	Deut 10–11
8	Mark 10:1–31	Num 17–18	24	Luke 1:57–80	Deut 12–14
9	Mark 10:32–52	Num 19–20	25	Luke 2:1–24	Deut 15–17
10	Mark 11:1–14	Num 21–22	26	Luke 2:25–52	Deut 18–20
11	Mark 11:15–33	Num 23–24	27	Luke 3:1–20	Deut 21–22
12	Mark 12:1–27	Num 25–26	28	Luke 3:21–38	Deut 23–25
13	Mark 12:28–44	Num 27–28	29	Luke 4:1–15	Deut 26–27
14	Mark 13:1–23	Num 29–30	30	Luke 4:16–44	Deut 28–29
15	Mark 13:24–37	Num 31	31	Luke 5:1–16	Deut 30–31
16	Mark 14:1–21	Num 32–33			

APRIL

DAY	NEW TESTAMENT	OLD TESTAMENT	DAY	NEW TESTAMENT	OLD TESTAMENT
1	Luke 5:17–39	Deut 32	16	Luke 12:1–21	Judg 7–8
2	Luke 6:1–26	Deut 33–34	17	Luke 12:22–40	Judg 9–10
3	Luke 6:27–49	Josh 1–4	18	Luke 12:41–59	Judg 11–13
4	Luke 7:1–17	Josh 5–7	19	Luke 13:1–17	Judg 14–16
5	Luke 7:18–50	Josh 8–9	20	Luke 13:18–35	Judg 17–19
6	Luke 8:1–18	Josh 10–12	21	Luke 14:1–14	Judg 20–21
7	Luke 8:19–39	Josh 13–14	22	Luke 14:15–35	Ruth 1–2
8	Luke 8:40–56	Josh 15–16	23	Luke 15	Ruth 3–4
9	Luke 9:1–27	Josh 17–18	24	Luke 16	1 Sam 1–3
10	Luke 9:28–45	Josh 19–20	25	Luke 17:1–19	1 Sam 4–6
11	Luke 9:46–62	Josh 21–22	26	Luke 17:20–37	1 Sam 7–9
12	Luke 10:1–20	Josh 23–24	27	Luke 18:1–17	1 Sam 10–12
13	Luke 10:21–42	Judg 1–2	28	Luke 18:18–43	1 Sam 13–14
14	Luke 11:1–28	Judg 3–4	29	Luke 19:1–27	1 Sam 15–16
15	Luke 11:29–54	Judg 5–6	30	Luke 19:28–48	1 Sam 17

Traditional Reading Plan

MAY

DAY	NEW TESTAMENT	OLD TESTAMENT	DAY	NEW TESTAMENT	OLD TESTAMENT
1	Luke 20:1–26	1 Sam 18–19	17	John 3:22–36	1 King 1
2	Luke 20:27–47	1 Sam 20–22	18	John 4:1–26	1 King 2–3
3	Luke 21:1–24	1 Sam 23–24	19	John 4:27–54	1 King 4–5
4	Luke 21:25–38	1 Sam 25–26	20	John 5:1–18	1 King 6–7
5	Luke 22:1–23	1 Sam 27–29	21	John 5:19–47	1 King 8
6	Luke 22:24–53	1 Sam 30–31	22	John 6:1–21	1 King 9
7	Luke 22:54–71	2 Sam 1–3	23	John 6:22–51	1 King 10–11
8	Luke 23:1–25	2 Sam 4–6	24	John 6:52–71	1 King 12–13
9	Luke 23:26–56	2 Sam 7–10	25	John 7:1–24	1 King 14–15
10	Luke 24:1–12	2 Sam 11–12	26	John 7:25–39	1 King 16–17
11	Luke 24:13–35	2 Sam 13–14	27	John 7:40–53	1 King 18–19
12	Luke 24:36–53	2 Sam 15–16	28	John 8:1–20	1 King 20–21
13	John 1:1–34	2 Sam 17–18	29	John 8:21–47	1 King 22
14	John 1:35–51	2 Sam 19–20	30	John 8:48–59	2 King 1–3
15	John 2	2 Sam 21–22	31	John 9:1–12	2 King 4–5
16	John 3:1–21	2 Sam 23–24			

JUNE

DAY	NEW TESTAMENT	OLD TESTAMENT	DAY	NEW TESTAMENT	OLD TESTAMENT
1	John 9:13–41	2 King 6–7	16	John 18:25–40	1 Chron 11–12
2	John 10:1–21	2 King 8–9	17	John 19:1–16	1 Chron 13–15
3	John 10:22–42	2 King 10–11	18	John 19:17–42	1 Chron 16–17
4	John 11:1–27	2 King 12–14	19	John 20:1–18	1 Chron 18–19
5	John 11:28–57	2 King 15–16	20	John 20:19–31	1 Chron 20–21
6	John 12:1–26	2 King 17	21	John 21	1 Chron 22–23
7	John 12:27–50	2 King 18–19	22	Acts 1	1 Chron 24–25
8	John 13:1–20	2 King 20–21	23	Acts 2:1–21	1 Chron 26–27
9	John 13:21–38	2 King 22–23	24	Acts 2:22–47	1 Chron 28–29
10	John 14:1–14	2 King 24–25	25	Acts 3	2 Chron 1–3
11	John 14:15–31	1 Chron 1–2	26	Acts 4:1–22	2 Chron 4–6
12	John 15	1 Chron 3–5	27	Acts 4:23–37	2 Chron 7–8
13	John 16	1 Chron 6	28	Acts 5:1–16	2 Chron 9–11
14	John 17	1 Chron 7–8	29	Acts 5:17–42	2 Chron 12–14
15	John 18:1–24	1 Chron 9–10	30	Acts 6	2 Chron 15–17

Traditional *Reading Plan*

JULY

DAY	NEW TESTAMENT	OLD TESTAMENT	DAY	NEW TESTAMENT	OLD TESTAMENT
1	Acts 7:1–19	2 Chron 18–20	17	Acts 16:1–15	Neh 10–11
2	Acts 7:20–43	2 Chron 21–23	18	Acts 16:16–40	Neh 12–13
3	Acts 7:44–60	2 Chron 24–25	19	Acts 17:1–15	Esth 1–3
4	Acts 8:1–25	2 Chron 26–28	20	Acts 17:16–34	Esth 4–6
5	Acts 8:26–40	2 Chron 29–30	21	Acts 18	Esth 7–10
6	Acts 9:1–22	2 Chron 31–32	22	Acts 19:1–20	Job 1–3
7	Acts 9:23–43	2 Chron 33–34	23	Acts 19:21–41	Job 4–6
8	Acts 10:1–23	2 Chron 35–36	24	Acts 20:1–16	Job 7–8
9	Acts 10:24–48	Ezra 1–3	25	Acts 20:17–38	Job 9–11
10	Acts 11	Ezra 4–6	26	Acts 21:1–14	Job 12–13
11	Acts 12	Ezra 7–8	27	Acts 21:15–40	Job 14–16
12	Acts 13:1–31	Ezra 9–10	28	Acts 22	Job 17–19
13	Acts 13:32–52	Neh 1–3	29	Acts 23:1–22	Job 20–21
14	Acts 14	Neh 4–5	30	Acts 23:23–35	Job 22–23
15	Acts 15:1–21	Neh 6–7	31	Acts 24	Job 24–27
16	Acts 15:22–41	Neh 8–9			

AUGUST

DAY	NEW TESTAMENT	OLD TESTAMENT	DAY	NEW TESTAMENT	OLD TESTAMENT
1	Acts 25	Job 28–29	17	Rom 9	Ps 39–43
2	Acts 26	Job 30–31	18	Rom 10	Ps 44–47
3	Acts 27:1–12	Job 32–33	19	Rom 11:1–21	Ps 48–51
4	Acts 27:13–44	Job 34–36	20	Rom 11:22–36	Ps 52–56
5	Acts 28:1–15	Job 37–38	21	Rom 12	Ps 57–61
6	Acts 28:16–31	Job 39–40	22	Rom 13	Ps 62–66
7	Rom 1:1–17	Job 41–42	23	Rom 14	Ps 67–69
8	Rom 1:18–32	Ps 1–6	24	Rom 15:1–21	Ps 70–72
9	Rom 2	Ps 7–12	25	Rom 15:22–33	Ps 73–74
10	Rom 3	Ps 13–17	26	Rom 16	Ps 75–77
11	Rom 4	Ps 18–21	27	1 Cor 1	Ps 78–79
12	Rom 5	Ps 22–24	28	1 Cor 2	Ps 80–84
13	Rom 6	Ps 25–29	29	1 Cor 3	Ps 85–88
14	Rom 7	Ps 30–33	30	1 Cor 4	Ps 89–90
15	Rom 8:1–17	Ps 34–36	31	1 Cor 5	Ps 91–94
16	Rom 8:18–39	Ps 37–38			

Traditional Reading Plan

SEPTEMBER

DAY	NEW TESTAMENT	OLD TESTAMENT	DAY	NEW TESTAMENT	OLD TESTAMENT
1	1 Cor 6	Ps 95–101	16	2 Cor 1	Prov 7–8
2	1 Cor 7:1–24	Ps 102–103	17	2 Cor 2	Prov 9–11
3	1 Cor 7:25–40	Ps 104–105	18	2 Cor 3	Prov 12–13
4	1 Cor 8	Ps 106	19	2 Cor 4	Prov 14–15
5	1 Cor 9	Ps 107–109	20	2 Cor 5	Prov 16–17
6	1 Cor 10	Ps 110–114	21	2 Cor 6	Prov 18–19
7	1 Cor 11:1–16	Ps 115–118	22	2 Cor 7	Prov 20–21
8	1 Cor 11:17–34	Ps 119	23	2 Cor 8	Prov 22–23
9	1 Cor 12	Ps 120–132	24	2 Cor 9	Prov 24–25
10	1 Cor 13	Ps 133–139	25	2 Cor 10	Prov 26–28
11	1 Cor 14:1–25	Ps 140–144	26	2 Cor 11	Prov 29–31
12	1 Cor 14:26–40	Ps 145–150	27	2 Cor 12	Ecc 1–3
13	1 Cor 15:1–34	Prov 1–2	28	2 Cor 13	Ecc 4–6
14	1 Cor 15:35–58	Prov 3–4	29	Gal 1	Ecc 7–9
15	1 Cor 16	Prov 5–6	30	Gal 2	Ecc 10–12

OCTOBER

DAY	NEW TESTAMENT	OLD TESTAMENT	DAY	NEW TESTAMENT	OLD TESTAMENT
1	Gal 3	Song 1–4	17	Col 3	Isa 45–47
2	Gal 4	Song 5–8	18	Col 4	Isa 48–50
3	Gal 5	Isa 1–2	19	1 Thess 1	Isa 51–54
4	Gal 6	Isa 3–6	20	1 Thess 2	Isa 55–58
5	Eph 1	Isa 7–8	21	1 Thess 3	Isa 59–63
6	Eph 2	Isa 9–11	22	1 Thess 4	Isa 64–66
7	Eph 3	Isa 12–15	23	1 Thess 5	Jer 1–2
8	Eph 4	Isa 16–19	24	2 Thess 1	Jer 3–4
9	Eph 5	Isa 20–23	25	2 Thess 2	Jer 5–6
10	Eph 6	Isa 24–26	26	2 Thess 3	Jer 7–8
11	Phil 1	Isa 27–29	27	1 Tim 1	Jer 9–10
12	Phil 2	Isa 30–32	28	1 Tim 2	Jer 11–13
13	Phil 3	Isa 33–36	29	1 Tim 3	Jer 14–16
14	Phil 4	Isa 37–38	30	1 Tim 4	Jer 17–19
15	Col 1	Isa 39–41	31	1 Tim 5	Jer 20–22
16	Col 2	Isa 42–44			

Traditional Reading Plan

NOVEMBER

DAY	NEW TESTAMENT	OLD TESTAMENT	DAY	NEW TESTAMENT	OLD TESTAMENT
1	1 Tim 6	Jer 23–24	16	Heb 7	Lam 3–5
2	2 Tim 1	Jer 25–26	17	Heb 8	Ezek 1–3
3	2 Tim 2	Jer 27–29	18	Heb 9	Ezek 4–7
4	2 Tim 3	Jer 30–31	19	Heb 10	Ezek 8–11
5	2 Tim 4	Jer 32–33	20	Heb 11	Ezek 12–13
6	Titus 1	Jer 34–35	21	Heb 12	Ezek 14–16
7	Titus 2	Jer 36–38	22	Heb 13	Ezek 17
8	Titus 3	Jer 39–41	23	James 1	Ezek 18–20
9	Philemon	Jer 42–45	24	James 2	Ezek 21
10	Heb 1	Jer 46–48	25	James 3	Ezek 22–23
11	Heb 2	Jer 49	26	James 4	Ezek 24–26
12	Heb 3	Jer 50	27	James 5	Ezek 27–28
13	Heb 4	Jer 51	28	1 Peter 1	Ezek 29–31
14	Heb 5	Jer 52	29	1 Peter 2	Ezek 32–33
15	Heb 6	Lam 1–2	30	1 Peter 3	Ezek 34–35

DECEMBER

DAY	NEW TESTAMENT	OLD TESTAMENT	DAY	NEW TESTAMENT	OLD TESTAMENT
1	1 Peter 4	Ezek 36–37	17	Rev 6	Amos 1–5
2	1 Peter 5	Ezek 38–39	18	Rev 7	Amos 6–9
3	2 Peter 1	Ezek 40–41	19	Rev 8	Obadiah
4	2 Peter 2	Ezek 42–44	20	Rev 9	Jonah
5	2 Peter 3	Ezek 45–46	21	Rev 10–11	Micah 1–4
6	1 John 1	Ezek 47–48	22	Rev 12	Micah 5–7
7	1 John 2	Dan 1–2	23	Rev 13	Nahum
8	1 John 3	Dan 3–4	24	Rev 14	Habakkuk
9	1 John 4	Dan 5–6	25	Rev 15–16	Zephaniah
10	1 John 5	Dan 7–9	26	Rev 17	Haggai
11	2–3 John	Dan 10–12	27	Rev 18	Zech 1–5
12	Jude	Hos 1–3	28	Rev 19	Zech 6–8
13	Rev 1	Hos 4–7	29	Rev 20	Zech 9–11
14	Rev 2	Hos 8–11	30	Rev 21	Zech 12–14
15	Rev 3	Hos 12–14	31	Rev 22	Malachi
16	Rev 4–5	Joel			

Chronological Reading Plan

JANUARY

DAY	OLD TESTAMENT	NEW TESTAMENT	DAY	OLD TESTAMENT	NEW TESTAMENT
1	Gen 1, 2, 3	Matt 1	17	Job 22, 23, 24	Matt 12:1–23
2	Gen 4, 5, 6	Matt 2	18	Job 25, 26, 27	Matt 12:24–50
3	Gen 7, 8, 9	Matt 3	19	Job 28, 29	Matt 13:1–30
4	Gen 10, 11, 12	Matt 4	20	Job 30, 31	Matt 13:31–58
5	Gen 13, 14, 15	Matt 5:1–26	21	Job 32, 33	Matt 14:1–21
6	Gen 16, 17	Matt 5:27–48	22	Job 34, 35	Matt 14:22–36
7	Gen 18, 19	Matt 6:1–18	23	Job 36, 37	Matt 15:1–20
8	Gen 20, 21, 22	Matt 6:19–34	24	Job 38, 39, 40	Matt 15:21–39
9	Job 1, 2	Matt 7	25	Job 41, 42	Matt 16
10	Job 3, 4	Matt 8:1–17	26	Gen 23, 24	Matt 17
11	Job 5, 6, 7	Matt 8:18–34	27	Gen 25, 26	Matt 18:1–20
12	Job 8, 9, 10	Matt 9:1–17	28	Gen 27, 28	Matt 18:21–35
13	Job 11, 12, 13	Matt 9:18–38	29	Gen 29, 30	Matt 19
14	Job 14, 15, 16	Matt 10:1–20	30	Gen 31, 32	Matt 20:1–16
15	Job 17, 18, 19	Matt 10:21–42	31	Gen 33, 34, 35	Matt 20:17–34
16	Job 20, 21	Matt 11			

FEBRUARY

DAY	OLD TESTAMENT	NEW TESTAMENT	DAY	OLD TESTAMENT	NEW TESTAMENT
1	Gen 36, 37, 38	Matt 21:1–22	15	Ex 21, 22	Matt 27:51–66
2	Gen 39, 40	Matt 21:23–46	16	Ex 23, 24	Matt 28
3	Gen 41, 42	Matt 22:1–22	17	Ex 25, 26	Mark 1:1–22
4	Gen 43, 44, 45	Matt 22:23–46	18	Ex 27, 28	Mark 1:23–45
5	Gen 46, 47, 48	Matt 23:1–22	19	Ex 29, 30	Mark 2
6	Gen 49, 50	Matt 23:23–29	20	Ex 31, 32, 33	Mark 3:1–19
7	Ex 1, 2, 3	Matt 24:1–28	21	Ex 34, 35	Mark 3:20–35
8	Ex 4, 5, 6	Matt 24:29–51	22	Ex 36, 37, 38	Mark 4:1–20
9	Ex 7, 8	Matt 25:1–30	23	Ex 39, 40	Mark 4:21–41
10	Ex 9, 10, 11	Matt 25:31–46	24	Ps 90, 91; Lev 1, 2	Mark 5:1–20
11	Ex 12, 13	Matt 26:1–35	25	Lev 3, 4, 5	Mark 5:21–43
12	Ex 14, 15	Matt 26, 36–75	26	Lev 6, 7	Mark 6:1–29
13	Ex 16, 17, 18	Matt 27:1–26	27	Lev 8, 9, 10	Mark 6:30–56
14	Ex 19, 20	Matt 27:27–50	28	Lev 11, 12	Mark 7:1–13

258 How to Read Your Bible & Enjoy It!

Chronological Reading Plan

MARCH

DAY	OLD TESTAMENT	NEW TESTAMENT	DAY	OLD TESTAMENT	NEW TESTAMENT
1	Lev 13	Mark 7:14–37	17	Num 17, 18, 19	Mark 15:1–25
2	Lev 14	Mark 8:1–21	18	Num 20, 21, 22	Mark 15:26–47
3	Lev 15, 16	Mark 8:22–38	19	Num 23, 24, 25	Mark 16
4	Lev 17, 18	Mark 9:1–29	20	Num 26, 27	Luke 1:1–20
5	Lev 19, 20	Mark 9:30–50	21	Num 28, 29, 30	Luke 1:21–38
6	Lev 21, 22	Mark 10:1–31	22	Num 31, 32, 33	Luke 1:39–56
7	Lev 23, 24	Mark 10:32–52	23	Num 34, 35, 36	Luke 1:57–80
8	Lev 25	Mark 11:1–18	24	Deut 1, 2	Luke 2:1–24
9	Lev 26, 27	Mark 11:19–33	25	Deut 3, 4	Luke 2:25–52
10	Num 1, 2	Mark 12:1–27	26	Deut 5, 6, 7	Luke 3
11	Num 3, 4	Mark 12:28–44	27	Deut 8, 9, 10	Luke 4:1–30
12	Num 5, 6	Mark 13:1–20	28	Deut 11, 12, 13	Luke 4:31–44
13	Num 7, 8	Mark 13:21–37	29	Deut 14, 15, 16	Luke 5:1–16
14	Num 9, 10, 11	Mark 14:1–26	30	Deut 17, 18, 19	Luke 5:17–39
15	Num 12, 13, 14	Mark 14:27–53	31	Deut 20, 21, 22	Luke 6:1–26
16	Num 15, 16	Mark 14:54–72			

APRIL

DAY	OLD TESTAMENT	NEW TESTAMENT	DAY	OLD TESTAMENT	NEW TESTAMENT
1	Deut 23, 24, 25	Luke 6:27–49	16	Judges 7, 8	Luke 13:23–35
2	Deut 26, 27	Luke 7:1–30	17	Judges 9, 10	Luke 14:1–24
3	Deut 28, 29	Luke 7:31–50	18	Judges 11, 12	Luke 14:25–35
4	Deut 30, 31	Luke 8:1–25	19	Judges 13, 14, 15	Luke 15:1–10
5	Deut 32, 33, 34	Luke 8:26–56	20	Judges 16, 17, 18	Luke 15:11–32
6	Joshua 1, 2, 3	Luke 9:1–17	21	Judges 19, 20, 21	Luke 16
7	Joshua 4, 5, 6	Luke 9:18–36	22	Ruth 1, 2, 3, 4	Luke 17:1–19
8	Joshua 7, 8, 9	Luke 9:37–62	23	1 Sam 1, 2, 3	Luke 17:20–37
9	Joshua 10, 11, 12	Luke 10:1–24	24	1 Sam 4, 5, 6	Luke 18:1–23
10	Joshua 13, 14, 15	Luke 10:25–42	25	1 Sam 7, 8, 9	Luke 18:24–43
11	Joshua 16, 17, 18	Luke 11:1–28	26	1 Sam 10, 11, 12	Luke 19:1–27
12	Joshua 19, 20, 21	Luke 11:29–54	27	1 Sam 13, 14	Luke 19:28–48
13	Joshua 22, 23, 24	Luke 12:1–31	28	1 Sam 15, 16	Luke 20:1–26
14	Judges 1, 2, 3	Luke 12:32–59	29	1 Sam 17, 18	Luke 20:27–47
15	Judges 4, 5, 6	Luke 13:1–22	30	1 Sam 19; Ps 23, 59	Luke 21:1–19

Chronological Reading Plan

MAY

DAY	OLD TESTAMENT	NEW TESTAMENT	DAY	OLD TESTAMENT	NEW TESTAMENT
1	1 Sam 20, 21; Ps 34	Luke 21:20–38	17	2 Sam 19, 20	John 5:25–47
2	1 Sam 22; Ps 56	Luke 22:1–23	18	Ps 64, 70	John 6:1–21
3	Ps 52, 57, 142	Luke 22:24–46	19	2 Sam 21, 22; Ps 18	John 6:22–40
4	1 Sam 23; Ps 54, 63	Luke 22:47–71	20	2 Sam 23, 24	John 6:41–71
5	1 Sam 24, 25, 26, 27	Luke 23:1–25	21	Ps 4, 5, 6	John 7:1–27
6	1 Sam 28, 29	Luke 23:26–56	22	Ps 7, 8	John 7:28–53
7	1 Sam 30, 31	Luke 24:1–35	23	Ps 9, 11	John 8:1–27
8	2 Sam 1, 2	Luke 24:36–53	24	Ps 12, 13, 14	John 8:28–59
9	2 Sam 3, 4, 5	John 1:1–28	25	Ps 15, 16	John 9:1–23
10	2 Sam 6, 7; Ps 30	John 1:29–51	26	Ps 17, 19	John 9:24–41
11	2 Sam 8, 9; Ps 60	John 2	27	Ps 20, 21, 22	John 10:1–21
12	2 Sam 10, 11, 12	John 3:1–15	28	Ps 24, 25, 26	John 10:22–42
13	Ps 32, 51	John 3:16–36	29	Ps 27, 28, 29	John 11:1–29
14	2 Sam 13, 14	John 4:1–26	30	Ps 31, 35	John 11:30–57
15	2 Sam 15; Ps 3, 69	John 4:27–54	31	Ps 36, 37, 38	John 12:1–26
16	2 Sam 16, 17, 18	John 5:1–24			

JUNE

DAY	OLD TESTAMENT	NEW TESTAMENT	DAY	OLD TESTAMENT	NEW TESTAMENT
1	Ps 39, 40, 41	John 12:27–50	16	Prov 16, 17, 18	Acts 2:22–47
2	Ps 53, 55, 58	John 13:1–20	17	Prov 19, 20, 21	Acts 3
3	Ps 61, 62, 65	John 13:21–38	18	Prov 22, 23, 24	Acts 4:1–22
4	Ps 68, 72, 86	John 14	19	Prov 25, 26	Acts 4:23–37
5	Ps 101, 103, 108	John 15	20	Prov 27, 28, 29	Acts 5:1–21
6	Ps 109, 110, 138	John 16	21	Prov 30, 31	Acts 5:22–42
7	Ps 139, 140, 141	John 17	22	Song 1, 2, 3	Acts 6
8	Ps 143, 144, 145	John 18:1–18	23	Song 4, 5	Acts 7:1–21
9	1 Kings 1, 2	John 18:19–40	24	Song 6, 7, 8	Acts 7:22–43
10	1 Kings 3, 4; Prov 1	John 19:1–22	25	1 Kings 5, 6, 7	Acts 7:44–60
11	Prov 2, 3, 4	John 19:23–42	26	1 Kings 8, 9	Acts 8:1–25
12	Prov 5, 6, 7	John 20	27	1 Kings 10, 11	Acts 8:26–40
13	Prov 8, 9	John 21	28	Eccl 1, 2, 3	Acts 9:1–22
14	Prov 10, 11, 12	Acts 1	29	Eccl 4, 5, 6	Acts 9:23–43
15	Prov 13, 14, 15	Acts 2:1–21	30	Eccl 7, 8, 9	Acts 10:1–23

260 How to Read Your Bible & Enjoy It!

Chronological Reading Plan

JULY

DAY	OLD TESTAMENT	NEW TESTAMENT	DAY	OLD TESTAMENT	NEW TESTAMENT
1	Eccl 10, 11, 12	Acts 10:24–48	17	2 Kings 17, 18	Gal 4
2	1 Kings 12, 13	Acts 11	18	2 Kings 19, 20, 21	Gal 5
3	1 Kings 14, 15	Acts 12	19	2 Kings 22, 23	Gal 6
4	1 Kings 16, 17, 18	Acts 13:1–25	20	2 Kings 24, 25	Acts 16:1–21
5	1 Kings 19, 20	Acts 13:26–52	21	Ps 1, 2, 10	Acts 16:22–40
6	1 Kings 21, 22	Acts 14	22	Ps 33, 43, 66	Phil 1
7	2 Kings 1, 2, 3	James 1	23	Ps 67, 71	Phil 2
8	2 Kings 4, 5, 6	James 2	24	Ps 89, 92	Phil 3
9	2 Kings 7, 8, 9	James 3	25	Ps 93, 94, 95	Phil 4
10	2 Kings 10, 11, 12	James 4	26	Ps 96, 97, 98	Acts 17:1–15
11	2 Kings 13, 14	James 5	27	Ps 99, 100, 102	Acts 17:16–34
12	Jonah 1, 2, 3, 4	Acts 15:1–21	28	Ps 104, 105	1 Thess 1
13	Amos 1, 2, 3	Acts 15:22–41	29	Ps 106, 111, 112	1 Thess 2
14	Amos 4, 5, 6	Gal 1	30	Ps 113, 114, 115	1 Thess 3
15	Amos 7, 8, 9	Gal 2	31	Ps 116, 117, 118	1 Thess 4
16	2 Kings 15, 16	Gal 3			

AUGUST

DAY	OLD TESTAMENT	NEW TESTAMENT	DAY	OLD TESTAMENT	NEW TESTAMENT
1	Ps 119:1–88	1 Thess 5	17	Ps 45, 46, 47	1 Cor 10:19–33
2	Ps 119:89–176	2 Thess 1	18	Ps 48, 49, 50	1 Cor 11:1–16
3	Ps 120, 121, 122	2 Thess 2	19	Ps 73, 85	1 Cor 11:17–34
4	Ps 123, 124, 125	2 Thess 3	20	Ps 87, 88	1 Cor 12
5	Ps 127, 128, 129	Acts 18	21	1 Chron 17, 18, 19	1 Cor 13
6	Ps 130, 131, 132	1 Cor 1	22	1 Chron 20, 21, 22	1 Cor 14:1–20
7	Ps 133, 134, 135	1 Cor 2	23	1 Chron 23, 24, 25	1 Cor 14:21–40
8	Ps 136, 146	1 Cor 3	24	1 Chron 26, 27	1 Cor 15:1–28
9	Ps 147, 148	1 Cor 4	25	1 Chron 28, 29	1 Cor 15:29–58
10	Ps 149, 150	1 Cor 5	26	2 Chron 1, 2, 3	1 Cor 16
11	1 Chron 1, 2, 3	1 Cor 6	27	2 Chron 4, 5, 6	2 Cor 1
12	1 Chron 4, 5, 6	1 Cor 7:1–19	28	2 Chron 7, 8, 9	2 Cor 2
13	1 Chron 7, 8, 9	1 Cor 7:20–40	29	2 Chron 10, 11, 12	2 Cor 3
14	1 Chron 10, 11, 12	1 Cor 8	30	2 Chron 13, 14	2 Cor 4
15	1 Chron 13, 14, 15	1 Cor 9	31	2 Chron 15, 16	2 Cor 5
16	1 Chron 16; Ps 42, 44	1 Cor 10:1–18			

Chronological Reading Plan

SEPTEMBER

DAY	OLD TESTAMENT	NEW TESTAMENT	DAY	OLD TESTAMENT	NEW TESTAMENT
1	2 Chron 17, 18	2 Cor 6	16	Isa 14, 15, 16	Eph 3
2	2 Chron 19, 20	2 Cor 7	17	Isa 17, 18, 19	Eph 4
3	2 Chron 21; Obad	2 Cor 8	18	Isa 20, 21, 22	Eph 5:1–16
4	2 Chron 22; Joel 1	2 Cor 9	19	Isa 23, 24, 25	Eph 5:17–33
5	2 Chron 23; Joel 2, 3	2 Cor 10	20	Isa 26, 27	Eph 6
6	2 Chron 24, 25, 26	2 Cor 11:1–15	21	Isa 28, 29	Rom 1
7	Isa 1, 2	2 Cor 11:16–33	22	Isa 30, 31	Rom 2
8	Isa 3, 4	2 Cor 12	23	Isa 32, 33	Rom 3
9	Isa 5, 6	2 Cor 13	24	Isa 34, 35, 36	Rom 4
10	2 Chron 27, 28	Acts 19:1–20	25	Isa 37, 38	Rom 5
11	2 Chron 29, 30	Acts 19:21–41	26	Isa 39, 40	Rom 6
12	2 Chron 31, 32	Acts 20:1–16	27	Isa 41, 42	Rom 7
13	Isa 7, 8	Acts 20:17–38	28	Isa 43, 44	Rom 8:1–21
14	Isa 9, 10	Eph 1	29	Isa 45, 46	Rom 8:22–39
15	Isa 11, 12, 13	Eph 2	30	Isa 47, 48, 49	Rom 9:1–15

OCTOBER

DAY	OLD TESTAMENT	NEW TESTAMENT	DAY	OLD TESTAMENT	NEW TESTAMENT
1	Isa 50, 51, 52	Rom 9:16–33	17	2 Chron 35; Hab 1, 2, 3	Acts 25
2	Isa 53, 54, 55	Rom 10	18	Jer 1, 2	Acts 26
3	Isa 56, 57, 58	Rom 11:1–18	19	Jer 3, 4, 5	Acts 27:1–26
4	Isa 59, 60, 61	Rom 11:19–36	20	Jer 6, 11, 12	Acts 27:27–44
5	Isa 62, 63, 64	Rom 12	21	Jer 7, 8, 26	Acts 28
6	Isa 65, 66	Rom 13	22	Jer 9, 10, 14	Col 1
7	Hos 1, 2, 3, 4	Rom 14	23	Jer 15, 16, 17	Col 2
8	Hos 5, 6, 7, 8	Rom 15:1–13	24	Jer 18, 19	Col 3
9	Hos 9, 10, 11	Rom 15:14–33	25	Jer 20, 35, 36	Col 4
10	Hos 12, 13, 14	Rom 16	26	Jer 25, 45, 46	Heb 1
11	Micah 1, 2, 3	Acts 21:1–17	27	Jer 47, 48	Heb 2
12	Micah 4, 5	Acts 21:18–40	28	Jer 49, 13, 22	Heb 3
13	Micah 6, 7	Acts 22	29	Jer 23, 24	Heb 4
14	Nah 1, 2, 3	Acts 23:1–15	30	Jer 27, 28, 29	Heb 5
15	2 Chron 33, 34	Acts 23:16–35	31	Jer 50	Heb 6
16	Zeph 1, 2, 3	Acts 24			

262   How to Read Your Bible & Enjoy It!

Chronological *Reading Plan*

NOVEMBER

DAY	OLD TESTAMENT	NEW TESTAMENT	DAY	OLD TESTAMENT	NEW TESTAMENT
1	Jer 51, 30	Heb 7	16	Ezek 3, 4	1 Tim 3
2	Jer 31, 32	Heb 8	17	Ezek 5, 6, 7	1 Tim 4
3	Jer 33, 21	Heb 9	18	Ezek 8, 9, 10	1 Tim 5
4	Jer 34, 37, 38	Heb 10:1–18	19	Ezek 11, 12, 13	1 Tim 6
5	Jer 39, 52, 40	Heb 10:19–39	20	Ezek 14, 15	2 Tim 1
6	Jer 41, 42	Heb 11:1–19	21	Ezek 16, 17	2 Tim 2
7	Jer 43, 44	Heb 11:20–40	22	Ezek 18, 19	2 Tim 3
8	Lam 1, 2	Heb 12	23	Ezek 20, 21	2 Tim 4
9	Lam 3, 4, 5	Heb 13	24	Ezek 22, 23	1 Peter 1
10	2 Chron 36; Dan 1, 2	Titus 1	25	Ezek 24, 25, 26	1 Peter 2
11	Dan 3, 4	Titus 2	26	Ezek 27, 28, 29	1 Peter 3
12	Dan 5, 6, 7	Titus 3	27	Ezek 30, 31, 32	1 Peter 4
13	Dan 8, 9, 10	Philemon	28	Ezek 33, 34	1 Peter 5
14	Dan 11, 12	1 Tim 1	29	Ezek 35, 36	2 Peter 1
15	Ps 137; Ezek 1, 2	1 Tim 2	30	Ezek 37, 38, 39	2 Peter 2

DECEMBER

DAY	OLD TESTAMENT	NEW TESTAMENT	DAY	OLD TESTAMENT	NEW TESTAMENT
1	Ezek 40, 41	2 Peter 3	17	Ps 83, 84	Rev 9
2	Ezek 42, 43, 44	1 John 1	18	Ps 107, 126	Rev 10
3	Ezek 45, 46	1 John 2	19	Ezra 5, 6, 7	Rev 11
4	Ezek 47, 48	1 John 3	20	Esth 1, 2	Rev 12
5	Ezra 1, 2	1 John 4	21	Esth 3, 4, 5	Rev 13
6	Ezra 3, 4	1 John 5	22	Esth 6, 7, 8	Rev 14
7	Haggai	2 John	23	Esth 9, 10	Rev 15
8	Zech 1, 2, 3, 4	3 John	24	Ezra 8, 9, 10	Rev 16
9	Zech 5, 6, 7, 8	Jude	25	Neh 1, 2, 3	Matt 1; Luke 2
10	Zech 9, 10	Rev 1	26	Neh 4, 5, 6	Rev 17
11	Zech 11, 12	Rev 2	27	Neh 7, 8, 9	Rev 18
12	Zech 13, 14	Rev 3, 4	28	Neh 10, 11	Rev 19
13	Ps 74, 75, 76	Rev 5	29	Neh 12, 13	Rev 20
14	Ps 77, 78	Rev 6	30	Malachi 1, 2	Rev 21
15	Ps 79, 80	Rev 7	31	Malachi 3, 4	Rev 22
16	Ps 81, 82	Rev 8			

... So they [the disciples] went out and fished through the night, but caught nothing ... Jesus shouted to them, "Throw your net over the starboard side, and you'll catch some!" And so they did as he said, and they caught so many fish they couldn't even pull in the net! Then the disciple whom Jesus loved said to Peter, "It's the Lord!" When Peter heard him say that, he quickly wrapped his outer garment around him, and because he was athletic, he dove right into the lake to go to Jesus! The other disciples then brought the boat to shore, dragging their catch of fish. They weren't far from land, only about a hundred meters. And when they got to shore, they noticed a charcoal fire with some roasted fish and bread. Then Jesus said, "Bring some of the fish you just caught." So Peter waded into the water and helped pull the net to shore. It was full of many large fish, exactly one hundred and fifty-three, but even with so many fish, the net was not torn. "Come let's have some breakfast," Jesus said to them. And not one of the disciples needed to ask who it was, because every one of them knew it was the Lord. (John 21:3, 6–12, TPT, addition mine)

Just after Jesus told seven of His disciples to cast their nets out on the other side of the boat for a historical catch, He brought them ashore, sat down with them, encouraged them, and made them breakfast. At Breakfast for Seven, we believe it's time for you to cast your net out on the other side.

BREAKFAST FOR SEVEN

breakfastforseven.com